About The Author

Elizabeth Ruiz CSCS is a strength and conditioning specialist who coaches athletes across a wide array of disciplines. With over 20 years racing experience as an elite road and track cyclist, Elizabeth garnered 11 Florida state cycling championship titles, as well as podium finishes in triathlon, duathlon, road and trail running events. With time spent in the racing trenches, she has firsthand experience of the challenges of preparation, travel, and race day performance.

Her coaching practice began as an offshoot from her role as bicycle fitting technician and coordinator for Andante cycles race team in Florida. While running training camps, Elizabeth realized the importance of having athletes properly fueled and wound up provisioning food and preparing meals for the cyclists and triathletes she trained. During her time living in Miami she incorporated the diverse tastes from the Caribbean, Middle East, and Latin America into her cooking repertoire.

Today Elizabeth resides in Wisconsin, working as a coach, designer, and freelance writer. She also cultivates gardens, hunts, gathers, and oversees the land conservation and wildlife habitat preservation on the family farm.

Dedication

There are many to thank for their part in this book.

To my husband Jaime who was my sounding board and companion for the shopping trips, the gardening, and general support I thank you.
Big thanks to my son Ben who would dutifully taste test, his help with photography, and for his willingness to share in the excitement of cooking.

A special shout out to my mother, a former home economics teacher, who led by example and shared the wisdom of great cooks such as Julia Childs, Graham Kerr, Mollie Katzen, and for the copy of "Joy of Cooking" she gave as a gift which is now tattered from years of use.

I cannot forget to recognize the influence of my pal Lynn Kellerman, who would endure hours in the kitchen preparing feasts and sharing in the passion of things gourmand, plus her sympathy for my frequent bouts of cycling induced road rash.

To my former sisters-in-law Gloria Botero and Celina Perdomo, and mother-in-law Socorro Orozco thank you for the excellent meals and opening up my culinary horizons. Despite the language barrier, they taught me how to make sublime Colombian food.

Thanks to Ben Greenfield for the opportunity to share this information with Endurance Planet and to Brandon Taylor for his editing and patience with this project.

Elizabeth Ruiz
EndurancePlanet.com

Table of Contents

Chapter 1: Why Eat Real Food?

Food sustains us, provides opportunities for social interaction, gives us pleasure, and even tantalizes us. But athletes think about food for more than its taste: food fuels us our greatest efforts and can be a determining factor in our level of race performance. Food can be a source of comfort after a hard workout and simultaneously an object of obsession for maximum improvement. From this concept of fuel and life improvement stems the term, "real food".

The mission of this book is to teach you how to prepare real food. I believe that real food can improve the quality of your performance, stabilize or improve your health through the rigors of training, and most importantly, satisfy the inner hedonist in you and make the trip to the table a source of pleasure, rather than a guilt trip.

In the world of food aficionados, the concept of real food has several levels of meaning. For clarification purposes, we will use the term real food to describe food sources that have gone through the fewest possible steps of processing and refinement. To illustrate, we will use two loaves of bread. One is commercially produced; the other is home made using more wholesome ingredients.

The mass-produced loaf of bread contains "industrial" ingredients commonly found in highly processed food such as refined wheat flour, hydrogenated fat, and preservatives to increase its shelf life. Although this bread can survive the test of time without spoilage, it has a rather weak texture and a consistency that allows you to roll it into a ball like putty. Not to mention the detriment those ingredients can have on your health. This loaf of commercially mass-produced bread has been fortified with synthetic vitamins such as thiamin, a nutrient lost through the milling process of the wheat when the bran is removed from the grain. You can tell things are bad when the bakers are putting things back in their dough to try to cover up the effects of their processing.

On the other hand you have a loaf of bread made at home or an artisan bakery using whole grains, yeast, butter, salt, and a few other ingredients such as honey or molasses. The real food version of your multigrain bread has a darker complexion, sporting a hearty texture due to higher bran content. It retains more of the original vitamin content found in whole grain compared to its white bread cousin.

This loaf of bread may have an alluring slightly yeasty smell, a coarser texture, and the best part of creating yourself: you know what ingredients it contains. If you were to fully embrace the real food movement, your ingredients would be locally produced grains, and other minimally processed ingredients such as sea salt, and honey from local bees instead of table sugar.

Real food is a way to pleasure your senses and promote local businesses through locally produced ingredients while providing a custom made source of energy to fuel up. Real food in endurance sports is a movement involving a slight shift of consciousness. Rather than relying on commercial sport food products, we promote a more sustainable way of staving off bonking on a long run or ride.

By producing your own food you can make an incremental step toward a more respectful choice in the food system. It's a win-win situation: save the earth while keeping the monkey off your back on your next long training adventure. By no means is this a suggestion to swear off using sport drinks or training gels on long training excursions. I only want to give you options and a degree of self-reliance and control.

An obvious answer to the question of why eat real food is that real food tastes better, and is more satisfying. Most people would elect to consume comfort food at the end of an arduous race, or after a hard training session as a reward, rather than dine on more gel packets or performance bars. Face it, for some people food is a near religious experience. It not only nourishes our physical needs, but it fills an intangible need of our spirit, and binds us together socially when shared with loved ones. The act of creating food and sharing with others can improve our mental state. Creative activities such as cooking, gardening, or even shopping elevate mood by increasing levels of dopamine, a neurotransmitter that gets switched on during rewarding experiences.

But there are other reasons to prefer making things yourself over buying that power bar. By integrating real food into our training table, and in our fuel bags, we can avoid potentially sabotaging gastric upset by using ingredients that work best for the individual athlete. Sayings like, "one man's food is another man's poison" don't become integrated into our everyday language without some truth to the origin of the idiom. All you have to do is look at food allergies, or serious disorders such as celiac disease where individuals cannot tolerate gluten. Not all athletes can function well eating the exact same food because even our organs don't look the same! The book, *"The Atlas of Human Anatomy"* illustrates that the human stomach has as many as 19 different shapes.

As athletes, improving performance in sport involves determining which foods work best for us. And as we gain a better understanding we avoid the pitfalls of selecting foods that cause gastric issues. By taking a more active role in our food preparation, we can hone in and practice using foods that allow us to perform better and more comfortably and possibly save ourselves from dependence on a retailer or availability of processed sport foods.

Face it, training and racing can be an egocentric activity. We leave our loved ones behind for early morning training, increase our carbon footprint by driving in our cars to training facilities or races, and litter the environment by leaving our shiny wrappers on the roadside. By working with real food, we can mitigate some of the "all about me" aspect of being a competitive athlete.

When we create our own meals and food for the go, we curtail the waste and costs associated with artificial foods. Who wants to use their hard earned money on packaging, marketing, transport, expired products, and other outside expenses associated with having the convenience of processed sport food?

We waste less when we use locally produced food ingredients in our own meals. You may not fix the hole in the ozone or global climate change by yourself, but every little bit helps.

Using relatively small adjustments in our routine, we can improve the quality of our nutrition, help local businesses, and move ever so slightly away from consumption without consciousness. If you wanted to become involved to a higher degree in sustainability, then the next steps in producing truly real food would entail shopping at local farmers markets, home gardening, organic gardening practices. You can even participate in local CSA's (Community Supported Agriculture) or hunt and gather if it is not against your ethical or moral fabric.

But do highly competitive athletes use real food? The answer is yes. Case in point is World Champion cyclist Thor Hushovd, who stands over six feet tall, and weighs 182. His build is much larger than the iconic pro road racer, and his caloric demand during a stage of the Tour de France can tear through 6,000 calories. According to an article in *Esquire* magazine, Thor's favorite food to eat on the bike is a ham and cheese sandwich. Off the bike he eats a gluten-modified diet comprised of a tasty variety of foods featuring curry dishes, vegetables, quality sources of protein and some traditional spaghetti. His breakfast features oatmeal, eggs, ham, rice, and cereal. When he's on the bike in competition he does eat commercial sport foods, but real food is included in his feedbag as well. His diet focuses less on wheat and other foods containing gluten to avoid the inflammatory effects associated with high gluten diets.

Ultra endurance runners rely on getting their calories from sources other than gels and sport drinks. Aid stations and special needs bags may contain potatoes, sandwiches, and fruit, in addition to sources of sodium in pretzels, chips or broth. In most long distance training or events, there comes a point when you crave comfort foods rather than squeezing another gel pack. This is where you begin to return to the roots of consuming real food.

Chapter 2: Logistics of Eating Real Food (the breakdown even if you aren't an epicure or chef)

One of the freeing things about eating real food is that it is a creative endeavor with almost limitless options. At the same time figuring out, "What's for dinner?" presents a decision making challenge that can drive one to desperation. And the last thing we want as real food eating athletes is to crumble by ordering pizza or hitting the nearest drive-through instead.

Just like training for a particular event or race venue incorporating real food items into your feeding routine requires some thought and planning. This book will provide you with recipes as well as tips for procuring and preparing the ingredients. Eating real food during training should be practiced and methodically approached just like one's training before using it on race day. Practice working with real food as you would for your training; your digestion needs time to adapt just as your muscles and cardiovascular system do.

Real food, *Morcella esculenta*, gathered during spring in natural wooded areas and is a gourmet's delight.

Is "Natural" Food Real?

Or is real food, "natural"? The real food movement involves a shift away from mass produced, industrialized food to the direction of sustainability, quality, and more wholesome nutrition. When on the hunt for real food, one needs to pay attention to labels that give the consumer the *impression* the product is wholesome or "natural so they will buy it.

Grocery stores and other vendors have little control over the packaging of their suppliers' products. Beware of the term, "natural". It is vague terminology used to window dress industrial food. Neither the U.S. Food and Drug Administration (FDA), nor the U.S, Department of Agriculture (USDA) has rules defining what is "natural". Conversely, there are strict standards for production methods of foods listed as USDA organic. For more information on the USDA's requirements for organic products   see

(http://www.ams.usda.gov/AMSv1.0/nop)
.

Production of organic food requires that a farm or facility be taken off standard practices utilizing chemical fertilizers, pesticides, hormones, and other chemical compounds used in some commercially run farms. This switch to organically certified practices can take years to fully transition over to. In the short run it can entail longer time for livestock or poultry to make it to market compared to standard practices. Organic meat, poultry and dairy are required to be free of specific chemicals such as growth hormones, and antibiotics. The extra measures entailed towards organic certification are one reason why choosing to purchase organic may cost more to the consumer.

The greatest benefits of organically derived food are in the long-term effects through sustainable farming practices. Organic farming has fewer damaging effects on the environment, lower health care costs to livestock predominately grazed on pastures, as well as slowing down dependence on fertilizers and pesticides. But remember there are opportunities to procure real food that isn't yet certified organic. Shopping from local smaller scale operations means you're buying food from places that aren't large enough to require artificial preservations and shortcuts.

Some foods available in the market such as onions, avocados, sweet corn, pineapples, mangoes, contain low amounts of trace pesticides and may not be worth the extra expense of selecting organic. Bear in mind that the practices used in commercial production of food may result in food that ships better over longer distances, has a more pleasing appearance, and shows fewer signs of insect damage. If you have ever seen an apple tree left out to its own devices, you would hardly recognize it you when it grew feral without the benefit of insecticides.

Organic food, especially meat, eggs, and dairy products can impart a more complex and stimulating palate due to diet of the animal. When cattle and dairy are raised free range on pasture they require fewer antibiotics in production, and have higher amounts of "good fats". The meat, milk, and cheese will take on the flavors of the grasses and plants that the animals graze on. For food connoisseurs, these intricate flavors are the very reason to opt for the real food option.

In addition to more complex taste, animals predominantly grazing on pasture versus grain result in higher levels of omega-3 fatty acids and conjugated linoleic acid (CLA) [1]. CLA is a compound found in meats and dairy raised predominately on grass. In scientific studies CLA has been found to have anti-inflammatory and anti-cancer properties, as well as having beneficial effects in maintaining lean body mass.

Where to tap into real food resources

You can get real food such as organic produce and meats in most grocery store chains. All it takes in a discerning eye to find products. The USDA has two distinct labels to identify foods with certified organic ingredients.

If you see either of these labels, you can be sure the product is at least 95% organic.

Figure 2.1   USDA labels certifying organic foods.

There are national chains of food stores specializing in organic food. Local food cooperatives in your community may carry a selection of organic food brands and locally grown produce in season. Some of the local produce may have organic origins, but have not yet obtained the stringent USDA certification. When in doubt, ask how it was grown.

But your sustainable options aren't limited to the common food outlets. You can buy at local farmers markets or directly from a producer. Buying local entails less travel to market, and fresher food that is in season. You can find out more about local food cooperatives, and farmers markets by searching on the Internet   at http://organicconsumers.org/btc/Buying Guide.cfm. Local produce can be found at grocery chains such as Whole Foods, food cooperatives, farmers markets and

Community Supported Agriculture (CSA's).

CSA's provide an opportunity for one to buy shares in a local farm in exchange for product. For your purchase of a farm share, you receive a portion of the harvest when the crops are ready and at their peak. In most cases, one can work on the CSA a few hours a week as a way participate in the food share without having to pay. This "sweat equity" allows the benefit of participating in the food production, in addition to working a few

hours alongside other share members who share the same interests in sustainability. If you are in a heavy training mode, working outdoors can provide a way to unwind, get dirty, and reconnect with the origin of real food.

If you have the available space, length of growing season and time, starting up a home garden can be another rewarding way to create your own real food. There is a time investment, and like your training, tending your garden requires maintenance. However, the reward of harvesting and preparing your own food can be worth missing a few races or logging in unnecessary junk miles. That reward is especially sweet when you consider the potential of tending a garden with your family. Just think of how fun and important kids will think real healthy food is when you involve them in a garden.

The beauty of growing your own is that you decide the scope of the project You could start a windowsill herb garden, growing tomatoes in a bucket, or go all out with a complex operation entailing raised beds and solar powered drip lines. Like your training, investing time into planning and program design will pay off with higher yields, less work, and fewer trips to the grocery store.

If quality food is important enough to get you starting up a garden, you may need to shift your competition schedule around to accommodate for the time you need to get your garden established. Find out when the last frost date is in your area, and block a few weeks off around it for your project. Digging manually or tilling can be hard work, even if you are an athlete. You don't want to overdo it by blowing out your hamstrings starting up a plot right before an important race. Check out local businesses that rent rototillers if you are planning on starting up a fairly ambitious project. I'm not saying everyone needs to do this. But if you feel strongly enough about a garden, this is the type of reprioritizing that it entails.

If growing your own food appeals to you and your family but you don't know where to start, contact your local state or county agricultural extension office. Make sure to look into 4-H group if you have kids who are interested.

You have your real food, now what?

The next challenge after getting real food is that not all of us enjoy preparing food, or have a kitchen that is fully equipped. Just as with athletic pursuits one can select an activity with a minimum of equipment and hassle, such as walking, or go the whole nine yards with technical aspects (racing time trials on a bike equipped with special cranks to record power output). The same concept applies to the kitchen.

You can prepare real food over an open fire with a cast iron skillet, or work on a range that rivals the cost of a cutting edge time trial bike. The investment of time and thought to your daily diet is worth it since nutrition plays such an important role in everyday athletic and mental performance. If you feel comfortable cooking real food the following section may just be a good refresher.

The Kitchen: where the magic happens.

Staples: items with a relatively long shelf life that you may use on a daily basis. Make sure you stock up on these. These items will be used almost on a daily basis when you decide to take control over your fueling by making your own

• Dried fruits and nuts: if you have sensitivity to sulfites you should be cautious with dried fruit, trail mixes, and shredded coconut. Check the ingredients. You can select raw nuts such as almonds, hazelnuts, and walnuts and roast them yourself, or using a food processor to make your own nut butter. Nuts in particular are a great source of energy for long endurance training. Because they are mostly fat, they will sustain you for longer aerobic rides and train your body to reserve glycogen stores.

• Cereals or grains: go for whole grain versions such as brown rice, wild rice, oats, bulgar, barley, quinoa, corn, and amaranth. Some of the lesser-known grains have a higher protein content than staples like wheat and rice. One note of caution regarding these real foods, because real hardly means harmless. Cereals and grains often have proteins called lectins which can inhibit nutrient absorption and cause gastric upset when consumed in large quantities. These lectins are completely natural defenses against extinction from animals eating them with abandon. Essentially they bind to your intestinal wall and disturb your gastric environment, making it more susceptible to ailments. But there is a way to combat the presence of lectins in grains. If you soak or ferment grains you can virtually eliminate lectins if you do it right. This often calls for soaking overnight and basically thinking ahead to get the most out of your food. In any case, you should check your individual sensitivity to grains because everyone is different.

If you use flour for baking, try to use up what you have in a few months. If you are concerned with insulin resistance or are eating a low-carb/ketogenic diet you can look into almond flour and other alternatives for baking. Just make sure you research the changes to recipe and cooking time you need to make if you use these.

• Dried or canned beans: variety is the spice of life, as beans are available in a wide variety. Combined with rice, beans provide complete protein for vegetarians. Dried beans are economical as a pound of dried beans can cost the same as a can, but deliver 3-4 times the amount product. The same advice about lectins applies with beans as well. But it is worth washing beans anyway to remove any impurities or any harmful residue from the canning process.

• Sea salt: if you are follower of trends such as the "paleo" or primitive diet try to find a sea salt from an area proximal to your genetic ancestors. Example: if your family of origin is mostly of northern

European descent, work with Celtic sea salt. If your ancestors were from the Mediterranean, then use sea salt from that geographic region. Sea salt contains a wider spectrum of trace minerals compared to regular table salt. Make sure if you rely solely on sea salt for sodium that you get adequate amounts of iodine in your diet through foods or via supplementation.

• Fats: grape seed oil, butter (yes, butter), coconut oil, olive oil, and even lard. You will need these fats to season your pans, and cook your foods. Sesame oil, walnut oil, and flax seed oil are used at cooler temperatures to flavor foods and to make salad dressings. Don't be afraid of eating fat, it's necessary for synthesizing fat soluble vitamins and keeping cell membranes healthy, among other benefits. For more information about the benefits of fat look at Ben Greenfield's Superhuman Food Pyramid, or Peter Attia's defense of fat.

Avoid using extra virgin olive oil at high temperatures and switch to butter, coconut oil, animal fat, or grape seed oil for those applications requiring the use of higher temperatures as less saturated oils denature at customary cooking temperatures. Extra virgin olive oil should be used for dressings, not for high heat cooking.

• Leavening agents: baking soda, baking powder. These ingredients provide texture and "lift" to baked items such as pancakes, biscuits, scones, and other quick breads such as cornbread. If you plan on baking your own bread, then invest in some yeast and store it in the refrigerator after opening.

• Herbs and spices: add flavor and interest to your food. Some herbs and spices have medicinal properties. For instance cinnamon has a great amount of fiber and is excellent for blood sugar and inflammation. If you don't plan on cooking often, purchase herbs and spices in smaller quantities since their flavor can diminish over time. As you venture through the recipe section of this book you will see a variety of herbs and seasonings that are called for.

• Vinegar: can be used to preserve and flavor food. Vinegar is derived from a wide variety of sources and can impart many flavors. Examples are cider vinegar, balsamic vinegar, rice vinegar, malt vinegar, and vinegar made from fruit juices.

• Sweetening agents: sugar is obvious, but there are plenty of viable sources of sweeteners that are real food. If you plan on making your own food and keeping tabs on the ingredients then consider alternatives such as honey, agave syrup, molasses, maple syrup, stevia, and raw sugar.

Weapons of Mass Consumption:

In this section, we are going to go through the kitchen step by step under the assumption that the reader has not a complete kitchen set up. The format allows you to go simple or more complex as you like. With a few pots and pans you are able to start taking control in making better feeding decisions. The most utilitarian way towards liberation from commercially prepared food is to start with a decently large skillet. If you are on a limited budget, a cast iron skillet is versatile, trusty, a source of iron in your diet, and gives you an arm workout when cooking.

• Skillets, pans. A word of advice, don't go with cheap or flimsy. Steer clear of Teflon or non-stick coated surfaces if you are concerned about possible health risks associated with non-stick surfaces at high temperatures. Learn how to "season" your pans to avoid depending on non-stick pans all together.

Pans can be seasoned, or made less prone to sticking, by first cleaning the surface to expose the metal of the pan. Next, heat up the pan in a hot oven at 300° for a few minutes. When the pan is fully heated throughout, coat the pan with oil or butter and then place the pan back into a hot oven for a half an hour or more. The oil will become polymerized onto the metal, forming a surface that prevents food from sticking. You may have to repeat this process more than once.

Avoid using seasoned pans to cook acidic food such as tomatoes, or vinegar, as it will degrade the polymer coating. When cleaning the pan strong cleaning agents should be avoided as soap or detergents will break down the seasoning causing foods to stick to the pan. Clean up can be done with hot water, or hot water combined with salt or baking soda and a little bit of elbow grease.

If you plan on cooking grains such as rice, quinoa, barley, and oats you will need a 2-quart sauce pan with a fitted lid. Larger pots, such a 4 to 6-quart capacity with lids should be oven-proof so that they can be used for roasting or baking in the oven. On the stovetop these larger pots can be used to heat up large quantities of water for cooking pasta.

• Good kitchen knives: Invest in a decent all-purpose knife such as a Santuko or chef's knife plus a sharpener. Detail work can be done with a paring knife. All knives should be kept sharp—the more blunt a knife is, the more dangerous. If you plan on baking your own bread, invest in a quality bread knife. Knives washed by hand will stay sharper longer, and the handle will go through less stress if they are kept away from the dishwasher.

• Cutting boards: note that the plural is being used. One should exclusively be for meat preparation and be washed using water at a higher temperature. The other should be reserved for fruits and vegetables. Avoid using wood cutting boards for meat and poultry as the bacteria can find a home in the cuts made in the wood from repeated use.

• Food Processor: if you are planning on making your own food often, and feel intimidated using knives, think about using a food processor. If you doing really involved cooking like making bread, processing your own nut butter, making condiments like pesto, mustard, or mayonnaise, consider using one.

• Measuring cups/spoons: critical for precision and accuracy if you want your recipes to come out anything like they are intended, especially when baking.

• Meat thermometer: again accuracy counts in cooking. You don't want to take chances consuming undercooked meat.

Fire

You can cook over fire, or in a civilized mode go with a simple hot plate. If you have a real kitchen most likely have a range, or oven. Technology provides a lot of options starting with a simple heated electrical coil to working gas. Most chefs prefer to cook with gas rather than electric since gas heats up faster and cools off right away when you turn off the flame. Ovens vary in technology, from a using gas, radiant heat, to convection and infrared.

• Pressure cooker: useful for beans and grains, especially good if you are cooking in a hurry. Pressure cookers shorten cooking time by using steam-generated pressure in a sealed pot. Items prepared in a pressure cooker require liquid. But if you're going to use one, make sure you watch it to prevent unattended explosions.

• Grill or barbeque: not really things to be used indoors but they appeal to the primordial attraction to fire. Best of all, the flavors of cooking over a grill cannot be replicated. A gas grill can save you from the hassle of waiting for your coals to heat up, plus saves a bit of time on clean up versus using a sauté or frying pan.

Hard core barbeque artists prefer working with real charcoal and wood to enhance the cooking flavors. Some grills such as the Weber™ brand use convection heating as seen by the dome shaped lid with adjustable vents. If you want to get really intricate there are techniques involved in cooking with fire such as grilling, indirect flame, roasting, and smoking.

There are over 600 titles offered on barbeque in Amazon.com, revealing the depth and passion of cooking with fire. One caveat to remember when grilling meat using direct heat is the formation of unhealthy chemical compounds that can form when meat is cooked at high temperatures during a flare up. These compounds are linked to diseases like cancer. If you decide to become grill master, then take the time to learn safe grilling techniques such as indirect heat method. Use a meat thermometer to check if your meat is safely cooked.

If you live in warmer climates and don't want the heat from cooking to heat up your living space, the grill can be a way to cut back on energy costs.

• Compost bin or bucket: pay it forward by using fruit and vegetable peelings, coffee grinds, ashes from the grill, combined with lawn clippings to build more productive garden soil. This is one more way to help save the earth by reducing waste entering landfills, as well as dependence on chemical fertilizers in home gardens.

Storage

By definition real, non-industrial, food doesn't have a long shelf life since it is free of chemical additives and preservatives. This means that once you buy your preservative-free food, you'll need to consume it before it spoils, unless it is fermented, brined, canned or dried. Examples of real fermented foods with longer shelf life would include yogurt and sauerkraut. These foods provide an added benefit as a source of probiotics: beneficial microbes that inhabit our gut and basically have the opposite effect of lectins.

Dairy

Check expiration date on the container. If you are storing raw milk, keep it refrigerated and use the product quickly— we are talking less than a week.

Cheese and yogurt has a longer shelf life (but not indefinite, unlike processed cheese food) due to the transformation carried out by microbes responsible for fermentation. Below is a suggestion of shelf life of a few food items (source: *Kitchen Companion*, USDA publication)

Product	Refrigerator	Freezer
-Eggs (in shell)	3-5 weeks	Only when beaten together
Eggs (whites only)	2 to 4 days	12 months
Eggs (yolks only)	2 to 4 days	Do not freeze
Hard-cooked eggs	1 week	Do not freeze
Ground meat	1-2 days	3 to 4 months

Fresh steaks(Beef, Veal, Lamb & Pork)	3-5 days	6-12 months
Fresh Poultry, Whole chicken or turkey	1-2 days	1 year
Chicken or turkey pieces	1-2 days	9 months
Soups & Stews: Vegetable or meat added	3-4 days	2-3 months
Leftovers	3-4 days	1 to 3 months

Basically when you have ground meat, cook and consume it quickly, or freeze what you don't cook right away. Ground meat, due its increased surface area, has a shorter shelf life.

Larger cuts of meat will last in the refrigerator longer, but to be on the safe side (and to enjoy them more), use up your purchases quickly. When in doubt, throw it out. The "sniff" test isn't worth the risk of making the wrong decision, and losing days of productive training time due to illness.

Oils

Oils need special handling and storage. Exposure to heat, oxygen, and light can cause undesirable changes to oil making it go rancid. Again, the smell test isn't going to help you identify when your oil has gone bad. Oils containing higher levels of polyunsaturated fat spoil faster. These include safflower, corn, sunflower, soybean, peanut, canola and olive oil. Sesame and flax seed oil have an even shorter shelf life. This is one reason why flax seed is sold in the refrigerated section of most natural food stores. When in doubt, refrigerate oil that isn't going to be used right away. Butter and spreads should be stored in the refrigerator as well.

Store your every day cooking oils in a colored container to block out light, or store them away from the light in an airtight container. Make sure to use the oil in a few weeks, just to make sure your oil is safe from going rancid.

Vegetables

If you purchase your vegetables from a local vendor in hopes of getting the "real deal" in farm produce, the next step is storing them properly. These guidelines are provided to save you from having your lettuce wilt quickly, or your potatoes go bad because you stored them with the apples.

Here are some very easy-to-follow guidelines:

- Cool and dry conditions: onions

- Cool and moist conditions: cabbage, rutabagas, root

vegetables, and potatoes (do not uncooked potatoes in store in refrigerator).

- Warm and dry: pumpkin, sweet potatoes, winter squash, dried hot peppers.

Frozen vegetables can last 3-months to a year in the freezer, depending on how they were prepared. Vegetables blanched at home from the garden can last up to a year if they are properly prepared.

Grains

Keep grains away from moisture, and free from insects or other animals. A metal can, bin, or glass container with a tight fitting lid works to store your grain. If your thinking about storing grains you've soaked then you need to dry them at a low temperature in the over so they don't get moldy.

Herbs

Try to use them up in less than one year. Spices and herbs can be preserved for later use by chopping them up and freezing them in unsalted butter, or water. Use a dedicated ice cube tray to freeze them, then store in a sealed freezer bag. Some herbs, such as rosemary, sage, cilantro, dill, and tarragon can be used to infuse vinegar. You may combine herbs and garlic into the vinegar solution. Store vinegar in a cool dark place.

Ease of preparation/Ease of carry/Ease of gratification

From least complicated to more complicated:

Meals ready to eat: MRE's

- Fresh and dried fruit, nuts, trail mix
- Prepared breads, tortillas with filling: sandwiches, roll ups, bean burritos
- Dried meat
- Salads: fruits, vegetables, nuts. Now you need a container and utensils

- Nut butters: make your own or check the label to make sure the ingredients are "real"

Foods requiring preparation: A glimpse at the start to finish timeline.

To prepare these items, you will need to actually start needing to cook. If you no longer have someone cooking for you may want to pay attention. Preparing your own food and having it prepared by a certain time is an exercise in time management. If you pick up a couple pounds of whole chuck, a bag of dried beans with some fresh beets, realize there is going to be a decent amount of time elapsed from preparation to hitting the plate. Just as racing events have different venues and durations, the same goes for preparing food.

Eggs: can be carried (as hard boiled) and prepared quickly.

Vegetables: can be served raw, steamed, sautéed, roasted, grilled.

Cereals, sides, porridge: rice, barley, quinoa, oats, Amaranth, millet. These items require water and moderately long cooking time. If you have soaked them you need to replace the water that now contains the extracted lectins.

Meats and Fish: you can do a lot with a skillet/sauté pan in a relatively short amount of time depending on the cut you are working with. Cuts like flank steak, skirt steak, ground meat patties can be broiled or grilled. Fish generally takes shorter time to prepare than red meat. Thicker, lean cuts, and tougher cuts of meat such as stews, roasts, and brisket can take hours to cook at lower temperatures.

Filets of chicken take less time to prepare than cuts with the bone in, and cooking an entire bird takes the longest. Ground chicken takes a short time to get fully cooked.

Legumes: Dishes as sides can be used as protein source for vegetarian. Can take more than 8 hours to prepare with soaking time if using dried beans. Cooking time for beans may take over an hour.

Breads: yeast requires time to work. Some types of breads require more than one session of rising. Baking can take time as well. General rule of thumb is a loaf of bread will take 3-4 hours from start to finish.

[1] Ha YL, Grimm NK, Pariza MW (1987). "Anticarcinogens from fried ground beef: heat-altered derivatives of linoleic acid". *Carcinogenesis* **8** (12): 1881–7. doi:10.1093/carcin/8.12.1881. PMID 3119246.

Real Food on the Go:
Alternatives to Consider.

There is a big difference between eating at the dining table, and what to consume during a workout or event. Food needs to be easily transported, and ready to eat while on the bike or during the run. The question arises, "can this be done without having to be dependent on commercially produced food?" The answer is yes, just as our ancestors were able to hunt and take nourishment with them, so can you break free of highly processed portable food. You need to practice to avoid any surprises on race day.

Incorporating real food items into your feeding routine requires planning, and practice. Below is a quick list of options for

• raisins, currants, and other dried or whole fruit

• bars or cookies

• sandwiches, tortillas, pancake "wraps" or ride waffles

• preserved fruit products: guava paste, honey,

• potatoes seasoned with salt or sweet potatoes mashed up in a food tube

The recipe section of this book contains instructions and details on how to create your own portable food as well as sit down meals.

Chapter 3: Breakfast Dishes

Simple and quick breakfast dishes will help fuel you for the most important meal of the day. If you are feeding before an event or intense workout, you may want to avoid eating a breakfast with heavy protein or fat content a few hours prior to your event. As you move through this section the recipes will become more complex in their preparation.

Eggs

Clean up and cooking is easier when you make sure the pan is well lubricated with oil or butter to prevent sticking, and the skillet is at the proper temperature.

Scrambled eggs
2	Eggs
2 Tb.	Milk or cream, or water
1-2 Tb.	Butter, or oil

Salt and pepper to taste.

Start with a well-seasoned skillet; heat up the pan on medium-high heat while preparing the eggs.

In a medium sized bowl place opened eggs and whisk with a fork until the eggs are lighter in color. Add milk continuing to whip. Hold the bowl at a slight angle and beat using fast strokes until the contents have gained a bit of volume.

Add oil or butter to the skillet. Test to see if the pan is hot enough by adding a drop of water .If it sizzles or "dances" the pan is ready.

Pour in eggs, turn down heat to low after a few seconds once the eggs have "set". Stir with a spatula every now and then, turning the eggs over to ensure uniform cooking.

Season with salt and pepper and enjoy.

Fried Eggs

A few minutes in the kitchen are worth the nutritional boost from eggs. Cooking time for fried eggs can be done in the time it takes to toast bread.

1-2   Eggs
1-2 Tb.   Butter, or oil. You want to add enough to cover the entire pan.

Start with a properly heated pan to the temperature hot enough to sizzle a drop of water. Add 1-2 Tb. of butter or oil allowing it to heat up.

Crack open an egg and pour into the skillet. Allow enough time for the white to go from transparent to white in color.

For sunny side up eggs, leave the egg on for another minute, and then serve.

For over-easy, flip over the egg and cook for another 30 seconds to the desired consistency is reached.

Serve with toast and fresh fruit.

Soft Boiled Eggs

Bring a small saucepan filled half way with water, 1/2 tsp. of salt, and 1-2 eggs. Bring the pan up to a boil. Let the eggs sit for 1minute before turning off the heat and letting the eggs coast and cook in the hot water for 3-5 minutes, depending on the desired consistency is reached. Drain water from saucepan and rinse eggs in cold water. Peel eggs or remove part of the shell and scoop out the contents.

Basic French Toast

Here is another easy and quick way to get fueled in the morning, or to reload after a long workout.

French toast can be made with french bread or hearty sprouted grain bread (this is preferred if you want to avoid lectins). If you use more rugged varieties of bread, you can soak the bread in the egg solution overnight to get a fluffier and softer version without having to resort to using white or french bread.

Ingredients
2	Large eggs
1/3 cup	Milk
2 Tb.	Butter or oil
4	Slices bread of your choice
1/4 tsp.	Vanilla extract (optional)
	Ground cinnamon as a garnish

Whip eggs in a medium bowl using a whisk or large fork. Add milk and vanilla, mixing until the ingredients are combined. If soaking the bread overnight, use a shallow dish to place slices of bread in and cover with milk and egg solution. Cover dish and place in refrigerator for 30 minutes to overnight.

If you are cooking the toast right away, have your medium sized skillet heated up so that a drop of water sizzles when placed in the pan. Coat pan with oil or butter until it melts.

Place the bread on the skillet allowing it to brown, around 4 minutes per side. Flip bread over using a spatula, cooking the other side until it turns golden brown. Sprinkle lightly with ground cinnamon as a garnish.

Serve with garnishes of your choice.

How to cook oatmeal and other grains
Microwave

When time is tight, and you need to multitask in the kitchen, the microwave can serve as a way to prepare oatmeal without having to constantly tend to the cooking process. For this method, use a heavy glass container, bowl, or large Pyrex™ measuring cup.

Ingredients
2 cups   Water
1 cup   Slow cooking /old fashioned oats (preferably soaked overnight)
pinch   Salt

Fill bowl with the suggested amount of water and cook oats on high for 2-4 minutes, depending on the wattage of your oven. The water needs to get hot. Add a pinch of salt, and stir in oats.
Then microwave at 50% power setting for 3 minutes or longer, so that most of the water is absorbed.

Let the oatmeal sit: it will continue cooking for a few minutes before serving. Add additional ingredients to the mix such as dried fruit, a touch of cinnamon or ginger, and lastly, nuts. Sweeten to taste with honey, brown sugar, or agave syrup.

Overnight method

Steel cut oats are known as pinhead oats, Irish oats, scotch oats, or coarse cut oats. They differ from rolled oats in that they are the inner portion of the oats that have been cut into smaller pieces, rather than flattened like rolled oats. Cooked, steel cut oats have a different texture, remaining chewy despite the long cooking time. This hearty version of oats works well when cooked up in a savory version as a side dish served with meats, poultry, or fish.

Basic preparation
4 cups   Water
1 cup   Uncooked Steel Cut Oats
pinch   Salt

Start with a medium sized pot. Fill with water, and heat up until the water starts to boil. Add salt and oats, reducing heat to low. Continue on low for 15-20 minutes, stirring occasionally if you want to serve them right away, or cook for 10 minutes and then allow the pot to cool before putting in the refrigerator overnight. Reheat before serving the following morning. Yields 4 servings/4 cups.

To doctor up and add excitement to your steel cut oats add:
• 1-2 tsp. ground cinnamon
• 1 tsp. vanilla extract
• fresh bananas, or other types of fruit
• frozen berries prior to reheating
• dried fruit and nuts
• ground flax seeds, chia seeds, sesame seeds, etc...

Breakfast Quinoa

Quinoa is a grain from South America that is high in protein and naturally makes a fine fuel for longer workouts. The method of preparation is similar to other grains, requiring water and a fairly long cooking time. Like the steel cut oatmeal, you may want to prepare this ahead of time, rather than losing out on training time in the morning.

Ingredients
2 cups   Milk (almond or coconut milk will work)
1 cup   Quinoa rinsed
1/4-1/3 cup   Brown sugar, or honey

In a saucepan, bring milk to boil. Add quinoa and let the mix boil. Reduce heat, cover, and simmer until most of the milk has been absorbed, around 15 minutes. Stir the quinoa to keep the texture fluffy.

Add to the cereal any sugar, or sweetener such as honey to taste and continue cooking until all the moisture has been absorbed by the grain.

Once finished cooking, you can add more ingredients such as fruit, nuts, milk, or yogurt. If using sweetened dried fruit, adjust accordingly on the amount of sweetener you use.

Granola

Add milk, or sprinkle on yogurt to make a meal rich in energy yielding carbohydrates, plus protein from nuts and seeds.

Pecan Granola
2 Tb.	Honey
¼ cup	Molasses
2 Tb.	Coconut oil (Melted)
½ tsp.	Ground cinnamon
½ tsp.	Sea salt

Mix these ingredients together so the ingredients are fully integrated.

In a large bowl combine:
3 cups	Old fashioned oats
1 cup	Sweetened shredded coconut
1 cup	Chopped pecans

Add the molasses mixture to the oats, coconuts and pecans. Mix well so that the granola is of a uniform color and consistency.

Preheat oven to 325°.

Spread out the granola mixture evenly onto a large rimmed baking sheet. Bake for 25-30 minutes, checking the mixture frequently to make sure it does not burn. Half way through baking time mix, and return to oven.

When baking time is finished, cool the granola for at least 30 minutes before storing in an air- tight container.

Cherry Granola

2 Tb. Honey
¼ cup   Maple syrup
2 Tb. Coconut oil (Melted)
½ tsp.   Ground cinnamon
½ tsp.   Sea salt

Mix these ingredients together so the ingredients are fully integrated.

In a large bowl combine:
3 cups   Old fashioned oats
1/2 cup   Raw sunflower seeds
1 cup   Sweetened shredded coconut
1 cup   Chopped almonds

Spread out the granola mixture evenly onto a large rimmed baking sheet. Bake for 25-30 minutes, checking the mixture frequently to make sure it does not burn. Half way through baking time mix and return to oven.

When baking time is finished, cool the granola for at least 30 minutes before storing in an air- tight container.

Pancakes

Below are recipes for a wide variety of pancakes with alternatives in the choice of ingredients. One of the most important aspects of successful pancake cooking is to have a well-seasoned skillet or griddle so that you can make several pancakes in one batch. Pancakes freeze well and can easily be reheated on medium power using a microwave. You can take pancakes with you on a ride, spreading your favorite topping on the pancake, rolling them up and wrapping them up for your fueling breaks.

Gluten Free Pancakes

Finding a gluten free pancake with the same texture as traditional pancakes is a challenge. These are fluffy, light, and exquisitely delicious pancakes. They offer a great alternative to gluten containing flours which can cause gastrointestinal, among other, problems.

Start with preheating your well-seasoned griddle over medium to medium-high heat. Have the oven set below 200° to hold pancakes while the rest of the batch is being made. Makes 8 6-inch pancakes. Ingredients:

1	Egg
1	Egg white beaten until soft peaks form
1 cup	Milk, or coconut milk
½ cup	Plain yogurt
¼ cup	Almond meal flour
1 cup	Gluten free flour
¾ tsp.	Xanthan gum
1 tsp.	Baking powder
1/2 tsp.	Baking soda

Using a medium bowl, separate the egg and beat the white using a whisk until soft peaks form.

In a large Pyrex™ liquid measuring cup beat the egg with a whisk or large fork. Add milk and yogurt, combining the ingredients well.

Add the flour, xanthan gum, baking powder and baking soda. Combine the ingredients, mixing until fully integrated. Fold in egg white to the batter, mixing using large strokes. Avoid over-mixing. Allow a few minutes for the batter to thicken slightly.

Pour approximately 1/3 cup of the batter

onto your pan. Allow batter to cook until bubbles near the center of the pancake form and pop. Flip the pancake, and cook the other side for 1 minute or longer as needed.

Coconut Flour Pancakes

These are fluffy, light, and exquisitely delicious pancakes. They offer a great alternative to gluten containing flours which can cause gastrointestinal, among other, problems.

Start with preheating your well-seasoned griddle over medium to medium-high heat. Have the oven set below 200° to hold pancakes while the rest of the batch is being made. Makes 8 6-inch pancakes.

4	Eggs
1 cup	Milk
1/2 cup	Plain yogurt
1/4 cup	Coconut flour
1 tsp.	Baking powder
1/2 tsp.	Baking soda

In a large Pyrex™ liquid measuring cup beat the eggs with a whisk or large fork.

Add milk and yogurt, combining the ingredients well.

Add the flour, baking powder and baking soda. Combine the ingredients and mix well, as coconut flour tends to clump. If the batter gets thick while you are cooking them, thin it out with a touch of milk, remixing the ingredients.

Pour approximately 1/3 cup of the batter onto your pan. Allow batter to cook until bubbles near the center of the pancake form and pop. Flip the pancake, and cook the other side for 1 minute or longer as needed.

Coconut Buttermilk Pancakes

Have pancake griddle heating while you combine the following ingredients:

4	Eggs
1 cup	Buttermilk
1/4 cup	Coconut flour
2 Tb.	Melted butter
1 tsp.	Baking powder
1/2 tsp.	Baking soda

Beat eggs until lighter in color. Add melted butter and buttermilk, mixing well before adding the dry ingredients. Combine flour, baking soda, and baking powder: blending until the batter has a smooth texture.

Pour approximately 3 tablespoons of the batter onto your pan. Allow batter to cook until bubbles near the center of the pancake form and pop. Flip the pancake, and cook the other side for 1 minute or longer as needed.

Rice Pancakes

This wheat free version of pancakes requires additional time to "cure" the ingredients before using the batter. You may want to start ahead the night before.

Ingredients:
1 cup   Cooked rice
1 cup   Milk
1 1/4 cups   Rice flour
1/4 cup   Brown sugar
2 Tb.   Applesauce
2 tsp.   Baking powder
1 Tb.   Butter

Using a blender or food processor, blend the rice, milk, and applesauce until the ingredients are creamy.

Add the rice flour, brown sugar, applesauce, baking powder, and blend in blender for 2 minutes. Let the mixture sit in the refrigerator for an hour to overnight

Grease a large skillet or griddle and place over medium heat. Pour 1/4 cup of the batter onto the griddle; cook until the underside is golden brown. Flip and cook until the other side is also golden brown, 2 to 3 minutes per side. Rice pancakes will take longer to cook than the wheat variety.

Spanish Potato and Egg Omelet (Torta de Patata)

This hearty rendition of omelet requires the use of a 12-inch skillet that can be easily handled and an oversized flat plate that is larger than the diameter of your skillet. Halfway through the cooking process, the omelet is flipped, and returned back into the skillet. This move requires a degree of skill in handling, but is worth the effort since this is an exceptionally satisfying dish that replenishes well after a long training session, or for a special brunch dish.

In the Spanish cooking tradition, you will be using olive oil, a lot of it. First you will be using it to brown your potatoes and onions, then to coat the skillet before cooking the eggs. To make this dish extra hearty, you can add precooked sausage (nitrate free) or chorizo. To make this dish stunning in presentation, prepare a bed of spinach greens for the omelet.

If you have never made an omelet before, read through the directions first before attempting this recipe. It is critical to have the pan properly seasoned, and heated to the correct temperature to avoid sticking.

Ingredients

½ cup	High quality olive oil.
3	Large potatoes (about 2 lbs.), peeled, and sliced into 1/8" thick rounds
½ cup	Finely chopped onion
4	Large eggs
1 tsp.	Salt

Heat skillet on medium high heat before adding two-thirds of the olive oil. Avoid overheating the oil to its smoking point.

Add the potatoes, carefully to avoid splattering the oil. The potatoes should cover the bottom of the pan, and the oil should cover the potatoes ensuring they will get cooked through. Flip the potatoes until they brown slightly and add the onions. Continue to cook for 10 minutes, stirring the food occasionally until the vegetables are tender. Transfer the contents once cooked to the large serving/ flipping plate, reserving the olive oil for cooking the eggs. Remove the pan from the heat so the oil doesn't start to smoke.

Using a whisk or electric beater, beat the eggs and salt until frothy in a medium bowl. Reheat the skillet and leftover oil to prepare the omelet. The oil should be hot, test using a piece of onion. If the onion starts to sizzle when dropped into the oil, it is ready. The pan should be covered with a generous amount of oil. Replenish with additional oil so that the entire cooking surface is well coated.

Once the oil has reached the proper temperature, have the eggs, vegetables, and optional precooked chorizo ready and on hand.

Pour the eggs onto the pan. Immediately afterwards, add the vegetables and heat for 2 minutes over moderate heat. Shake the pan to prevent sticking, making sure the entire omelet has some give and moves across the pan's cooking surface. When the omelet is firm, but not dry, cover the skillet with the large plate. Place one hand on the plate, the other holding the panhandle. Invert the plate while keeping the pan in contact with the plate. If performed correctly, the omelet will be on the plate. Return the pan to the heat, checking that there is sufficient oil on the pan so that when the omelet is returned to the pan the eggs will not stick. Carefully return the omelet back to the pan. Cook for 3 more minutes, allowing the underside to cook.

Serve at once.

Ride Waffles

More complex than pancakes, these waffle recipes require a waffle maker. Waffles make great portable food when you liven them up with jam, honey, or nut butter.

In Holland, the stroopwafel is a treat consumed with tea. Unlike Belgian waffles, which are technically "quick breads" due to the use of baking soda and or baking powder, stroopwafels use yeast as a leavening agent. Stroopwafels are prepared in special waffle presses called a pizzelle iron.

The following recipe works with a regular waffle iron. You'll need to allot time for the dough to rise and may want to prepare these ahead of time.

To prepare them as mobile food, cut waffles in half if you don't have access to a pizzelle iron, which makes a thinner, crispy waffle.

The traditional way to prepare these is to sandwich 2 waffles with a special filling made with a generous amount of butter, sugar, and corn syrup. Trying to keep these on the healthy side, the directions for the traditional filling will be omitted.

Instead of using 2 waffles prepared in a pizzelle iron, cut one waffle made in a Belgian waffle, or traditional waffle maker and fill with your choice of filling.

Ingredients
1 cups	Coconut flour
1/2 tsp.	Ground cinnamon
1/2 cup	Sugar
1 cup (2 sticks)	Unsalted butter
6	Large eggs
1	Package yeast, or 2 1/4 tsp. yeast
1 cup	Warm water, between 120-130°F
1/2 cup	Milk (just in case the batter needs more liquid)

Start by dissolving the yeast in warm water. Allow the yeast to get slightly foamy.

Meanwhile, in a large bowl, or standing mixer, cut the butter into small pieces and integrate the flour using a spoon, fork, or pastry blender until the butter chunks are the size of small peas. Mix in the sugar, cinnamon, eggs and yeast mixture until the mixture is consistent and uniform in texture.

Set aside the bowl in a warm place, and cover with a dishcloth or plastic wrap for 30-60 minutes allowing the dough to rise.

Divide the dough into 12 even portions, and roll into balls. Preheat the waffle iron and coat with oil to prevent sticking. Press the dough into the waffle maker, and cook until the edges start to brown and crisp. Cooking time will vary, depending on your waffle iron. If fortunate enough to have a pizzelle iron, bake for around 30 seconds.

Cut waffles in half and fill with your choice of fillings below:
• honey
• jelly or jam thinned slightly with warm water
• slices of guava paste and cream cheese
• Nutella, peanut butter, almond butter

and jelly
• mashed bananas
• agave nectar
• finely diced nuts or dried fruit with your choice of syrup, cream cheese, or honey.

Experiment to find out what your preferences are, and which combinations travel best. Wrap waffles in aluminum foil, wax paper, or similar before heading out on your ride.

Rice Waffles

If you are on the quest for a wheat free waffle, the following recipe uses cooked rice. In addition to using a waffle iron, a blender will be needed to incorporate the cooked rice with the liquid ingredients.

This recipe is taken from "The Feed Zone Cookbook" by Biju Thomas and Allen Lim and is a variation of the rice pancake recipe. Make these ahead of your next long ride and/or freeze.

Have waffle iron preheating.

Ingredients:

2 rice	Cups cooked white or brown
3	Eggs
1	Banana (almost over-ripened)
2 Tb.	Molasses
2 Tb.	Rice flour

1/2-1 cup Milk (if using white rice you may need to use more than brown rice)

Mix the eggs first to break the yolks, integrating the yolks and whites before adding them to the blender. Combine the cooked rice, eggs, banana, molasses and flour in the blender. Gradually add milk so that the batter is consistent in texture and thick enough to resemble traditional waffle batter. Pour slightly less than enough to cover the area of the waffle iron since the batter will spread out.

Cook in the waffle maker, until no more steam escapes from the waffle maker and the edges start to crisp. Store waffles in a warm oven, covered with dish towel until serving time. Set aside and cool for use as a ride waffle. Cut waffles in half, similar to the stroopwafel recipe and fill with similar fillings. Wrap in wax paper to separate waffles before freezing in sealable plastic bins, or freezer safe plastic bags.

Chapter 4: Real Portable Food

Snack bars are the staple food for training rides. They can even sustain us while we are on the go taking care of business outside of our world of training and racing.

You will find that after the initial investment of procuring ingredients that you can churn out batches of these bars without having to run to a retailer, and then you can tweak the ingredients to suit your tastes.

Note that on some of these recipes there are variations and alternatives, giving you the flexibility to pick your own ingredients for your own custom made creations.

For several of these recipes you'll need a food processor to help break down nuts, or dried fruits and to combine the ingredients, and a glass baking pan.

Carrot Cake Bar

A real food alternative to purchased bars.
Makes 3 bars.
Ingredients

1/3 cup	Rolled oats
¼ cup	Raisins
1/3 cup	Shredded unsweetened coconut
1/3 cup	Dried pineapple
3	Pitted dates
2	Medium carrots shredded
1/3 cup	Hazelnuts, filberts, or walnuts
1 tsp.	Ground cinnamon
½ tsp.	Pumpkin pie spice
½ tsp.	Ground ginger

Blend oats in food processor or blender until it is powdery. Add dates, and blend. Next add the carrots, pineapple and raisins, blending with each ingredient. Add spices, blending and combining all the ingredients. If the mixture is too wet, add more oats. If the mixture is too dry, add a touch of honey until the dough can be formed without crumbling apart.

Divide the dough into 2" x 1" pieces, cover with plastic wrap and let sit to cure and harden up in the refrigerator for 2 to 3 hours.

Protein Bars

Use an 8 x 8 inch baking dish to form these bars in addition to a food processor to do the hard work of chopping and blending. If you want to add optional chocolate you will need to melt it in a small thick walled sauce pan.

Ingredients

2 cups	Raw or slightly roasted almonds
1/2 cup	Ground flax seeds, chia seeds, or pumpkin seeds
1/2 cup	Raisins, currants, dried dates
1/2 cup	Shredded unsweetened coconut
1/2 cup	Unsalted peanut or almond butter
1/2 cup	Melted coconut oil
2 tsp.	Vanilla extract
1/2 tsp.	Sea salt
3 Tb.	Honey
4 ounces	Dark chocolate* optional

Prepare the almonds, flax seeds, dried fruit, and coconut by processing them in the food processor until they are coarsely ground. Add almond butter, salt and mix.

In a small sauce pan, melt coconut oil over low heat until it becomes liquid. Stir in honey and vanilla extract.

Combine the melted coconut oil with the nuts and fruit, working with a few pulses in the food processor until it forms a coarse paste. Spoon the mixture into the 8 x 8 inch baking dish, letting it chill for 1 hour in the refrigerator.

Using a small saucepan melt the chocolate over low heat, stirring frequently so that the chocolate does not burn. When melted, spread over the bars and return the baking dish to the refrigerator for an additional 30 minutes, or until the chocolate hardens. Cut into bars, then wrap individual bars in freezer paper, or wax paper. Store in cool, dry area, or freeze. Yields about 12-16 bars.

No-bake bars

These are simple to make, and you can add protein powder to increase the protein content.

Ingredients

1 cup	Almond, cashew, or peanut butter
1 cup	Honey
3 cups	Rolled, or old-fashioned oats
½ cup	Protein powder (optional)

In a medium-sized saucepan warm the nut butter and honey over low to medium heat until it mixes and is creamy in texture. Make sure your pan is large enough to fit the oats.

Mix in oats and optional protein powder. Turn off the heat, mixing until the ingredients are combined.

Press into a 8" x 8", or 9" x 9" glass baking dish. Let cool before cutting into 16 bars.

Savory rice cakes

Variation based on the Cashew and Bacon Rice Cake recipe from "The Feed Zone Cookbook" written by Biju Thomas and Allen Lim.

This recipe has a salty flavor component, as well as higher protein content for longer training sessions. Plus it features bacon, an ingredient not found in commercial bars and a refreshing change in taste. If possible use a nitrate free, or uncured source of bacon.

You will need to have on hand 2 cups of cooked medium grain, or sticky rice prepared ahead of time. The remaining ingredients will be mixed and then pressed into a 8" x 8" or 9" x 9" pan.

2 cups   Rice such as jasmine, or medium-grain rice.
3 cups   Water

Cook rice according to the directions on the package.

Meanwhile prepare:

8 ounces bacon. Instead of using the traditional stove top method, try this method of bacon preparation that frees you up from having to be at constant attention while the bacon cooks on the stovetop.

Preheat oven to 300°, or if using convection, 275°. Using a broiler pan lay out your strips of bacon on the sheet, making sure the bacon doesn't overlap. Bake for 15-30 minutes until the bacon is crispy, depending on the thickness of the bacon.

Blot bacon using paper towels to absorb extra fat, crumble bacon into small pieces.

Prepare two eggs. Scrambling them first, and sautéing them using a well seasoned pan over medium heat. Stir the eggs occasionally to prevent sticking.

Mix together in a bowl with the rice, bacon, and eggs along with the following ingredients:

1/4 cup   Nut butter of your choice
1/2 cup   Cashews
2 Tb.   Toasted sesame seeds
1/2 cup   Raisins, dried currants, or dried
cranberries

Press the mixture into your square dish, let cool in the refrigerator and cut into squares. Wrap individual pieces in wax paper, butcher paper, or plastic wrap.

Chapter 5: Soups and Appetizers

There is a reason why support foods in ultra long distances such as the ironman™ go from sweet to salty and savory as the race progresses. Besides providing electrolytes that are lost through sweat, this switch to foods like broth also breaks up the monotony of sweet carbs. You can only handle energy gels for so long!

In some cultures broth is considered to have curative powers—especially with the precious marrow inside the bone. But more commonly in the western diet broth or stock from economical cuts of meat and bones is the base for soups. Broth is good source of the minerals calcium, magnesium, and phosphorous. Bones with joints that are used in broth have ample amounts of arginine and glycine in their gelatin: proteins which allow the body to optimize protein consumption. This protein sparing effect of gelatin allows better utilization of protein for recovery and repair. Since the nutrients in broth are readily available, it becomes a go to food for rejuvenation and healing.

So there's your health benefit: ease in assimilation. But for your inner hedonist, the taste is *vastly* superior to canned soup. Stock is also prepared in large batches, so what you don't use right away can be frozen in ice cube trays then stored in a freezer bag for later use.

Basic Soup Stock Recipe

How to build your own stock: For preparing an all-purpose stock start with bones, chicken, turkey, or beef soup bones. You'll need cold water, a large stockpot, and a strainer. For one quart of water, you'll need two pounds of bones for rich delicious stock; 8 pounds of bones would make a gallon of stock.

To make a quart of all-purpose soup stock:

2 lbs. or similar	Soup bones, chicken skeleton,
32 oz.	Water
1 chunks	Carrot broken into 2 to 3-inch
2	Cloves garlic smashed
1/2	Medium onion quartered
1	Stalk of celery
1-2	Sprigs of fresh or dried thyme
1-2	Sprigs of parsley
1	Bay leaf
3-5	Whole peppercorns
	Sea salt

Fill stockpot with bones and water. Gently simmer for 30-40 minutes. Add carrot, onion, garlic, and herbs. Continue to simmer for 1-3 hours, depending on how flavorful you want your soup. Season stock with salt to taste after it has cooked. Make small adjustments as you go to avoid over-seasoning. If you want clear stock, allow stock to cool and skim off the congealed fat. Use a strainer to remove small bones, cooked vegetables, and herbs. Use right away, or allow stock to cool before freezing.

Vegetable Broth

Vegetables are an excellent source of minerals in a form that is easily digested. There are no set rules on which ingredients to use to create a vegetable stock. A suggested ratio of vegetables to water is 4 cups of vegetables to make 2 quarts of stock. Onions, garlic, carrots and celery are the base ingredients to start with. An example would be:

2-3	Stalks Celery
1	Medium onion
2	Carrots
2-3	Cloves garlic, crushed
2-3	Sprigs of fresh or dried thyme
2-3	Sprigs of parsley, cilantro, Italian parsley,
1	Bay leaf
3-5	Whole peppercorns
	Sea salt

From here you can modify your stock to contain a wide variety of vegetables such as: potatoes, parsnips, squash, mushrooms, green beans, bell peppers, leeks, scallions, chard, kale, tomatoes, etc.

How to do it:

In a large stockpot fill with one gallon cool water, adding celery, onion, carrots, and denser vegetables that take longer to cook first, such as potatoes and squash. Set the heat to high. After 10-15 minutes add garlic and then herbs and smaller structured vegetables last. Allow the water to boil, after a minute or two reduce the temperature to low and simmer for an additional hour.

Stir on occasion, adding salt to taste. When cooking time is completed, let the stock to cool a bit and strain. Allow the stock to cool significantly before freezing.

Egg Drop Soup

The best way to start a delicious soup is to create your own stock using lesser cuts of meat, or bony parts such as leftover chicken bones, with a few vegetables. Combine with the "perfect food" egg, and you have a nutritious warm meal. If pressed for time, use boxed stock instead. If desperate, use bouillon cubes mixed with water. If using homemade stock, you will need to add generous amounts of salt, keep adding and testing for the appropriate amount.

Ingredients

4 cups	Stock, or broth
1	Large Egg
1 Tb	Water
1/4 tsp.	Ground ginger
1/8-1/4 tsp.	Ground garlic powder
	Green onions as garnish

Measure out the stock into a medium sized saucepan and turn on medium heat. Add the ginger and garlic powder to the stock and heat up to a boil. Turn down heat and prepare the egg.

Using a small liquid measuring cup crack an egg and beat until lighter in color, add the tablespoon of water and continue to mix with a fork or whisk.

Using a large spoon, stir the soup base in the pot. While the soup is twirling inside the pan, pour the egg solution slowly while keeping the soup moving inside the pan. By pouring the eggs in a thin stream you will get thinner threads of cooked egg, rather than clumps.

Turn off heat. Garnish soup with thinly sliced green onions or scallions. Serve immediately.

Black Bean Soup

This soup is rich in sustained energy via the complex carbohydrates from beans, as well as a source of protein for vegetarian diets. When served with brown rice, you have a vegan meal with a complete source of protein. This soup is deliciously complimented with avocado, providing excellent fats for well-fueled endurance days.

Ingredients

2 Tb	Olive oil, coconut oil, or butter
1	Medium onion, diced
1	Yellow, green, or red bell pepper chopped
3	Cloves garlic minced
2	15-ounce cans black beans
14 oz.	Broth
1 cup	Naturally smoked, nitrate free cooked ham (optional)
1 tsp.	Cumin
1/2 tsp.	Sea salt

Ground cayenne, chipotle, adobo, or ancho pepper to taste.

Fresh cilantro, sour cream, grated cheese, sliced scallions as garnish.

Directions

In a deep pan, heat up oil over medium heat. Add the pepper and onion, letting the pepper brown just a bit, and the onion turn translucent. Add the garlic, sautéing for a few minutes to release the flavor. Stir in **half** the beans and **half** the broth, allowing the ingredients to heat up.

In a blender, or food processor, puree the rest of the beans and remaining broth. Add blended mixture to the soup mixture in the pot, increase heat so that the soup gets slightly bubbly, but not to the boiling point. Reduce heat, adding the optional ham, cumin, ground pepper, and salt. Let simmer for 15-20 minutes, and serve.

Roasted Cauliflower Soup

Cauliflower is caramelized in the roasting process, giving it a unique flavor while shortening the cooking time of soup made with this cruciferous cancer fighting super food.

Ingredients

2 heads	Cauliflower
2 Tb.	Olive oil
½	Medium onion, chopped
3	Cloves garlic, chopped
3 cups	Stock, or vegetable broth
1 cup	Water
¼ cup	Cream or whole milk
1	Bay leaf
	Pepper

Roasting the cauliflower:

Preheat oven to 400°. Prepare a flat baking sheet by lining with parchment paper.

Divide the heads of cauliflower into 2-inch florets and place into a large bowl. Drizzle oil over florets, season lightly with fresh ground pepper. Place florets onto parchment paper and roast in the oven for 20-30 minutes, or until golden.

Prepare the soup base by sautéing the onions in oil over a saucepan on medium heat for a few minutes. When the onions become a touch clear, add garlic. Add the roasted florets, stock, bay leaf and continue to cook over until the cauliflower becomes soft and tender, around 30 minutes. Add the milk or cream. Turn off heat, remove bay leaf and allow the soup to cool down a bit. Transfer soup to a blender or food processor to puree in smaller batches. You may also blend the soup using an immersion blender. Reheat before serving.

Thai Lettuce Wraps (Miang Kum)

This Thai appetizer features a diverse combination of flavors, with the crunch of chopped peanuts. Coconut milk adds a silky texture, as well as an excellent source of medium-chain triglycerides for sustained energy. You may have to provision some curry seasonings, fish sauce, coconut milk, and galangal at an Asian food specialty store. Use fresh ginger root if galangal isn't available. Serves 8-12 rolls.

Ingredients
1 cup   Cooked shrimp (see directions below if using fresh shrimp)
1/3 cup   Dry shredded unsweetened coconut
1   Head romaine lettuce
1/3 cup   Dry roasted cashews, ground or finely chopped
2   Scallions, sliced in very thin across the stem
2   Cloves garlic, minced or
2 tsp.   Grated galangal, or ginger
1/4 tsp.   Dried chili flakes, or 1 tsp. fresh chili
1/2 tsp.   Regular chili powder

1/4 tsp.	Brown Sugar
1 Tbsp.	Fish sauce
3 Tbsp.	Coconut milk
1/2 to 1	Fresh lime, sliced into wedges
1/3 cup	Cilantro, chopped as a garnish

Cook and prepare the shrimp, cutting it into pieces small enough to work as a sandwich filling.

If using pre-cooked shrimp instead of fresh cooked, remove excess moisture by draining or squeezing shrimp in a towel first. Chop until the consistency resembles coarse grain. Place shrimp in a mixing bowl and set aside.

(Directions for fresh shrimp) If working with fresh shrimp, first peel the shrimp, and if the shrimp are large enough to have a central vein, remove the contents before cooking the shrimp.

The actual cooking time of fresh shrimp is very brief, overcooking should be avoided.

Preheat medium sized pan over medium heat. Add a touch of butter or oil to the pan, allowing for the oil to reach cooking temperature.

Place shrimp on pan, cooking 1 minute per side, or until the color of the meat changes to a pink hue, adding more time for larger sized shrimp. Let them cool a bit before chopping into smaller pieces, and set aside in a mixing bowl.

Bring the same pan to medium high heat, and toast the coconut, stirring it constantly to ensure even browning. When the coconut color changes to a golden brown hue remove the coconut from heat and transfer to a bowl. Let cool.

Chop and prepare the green onions, garlic, and ginger if working with fresh ginger root. Mix with the chili powder, sugar, ground cashews, and fish sauce. Toss in bowl with the diced shrimp. Add coconut milk and stir. When the mix is integrated add the toasted coconut, leaving a bit aside as the a garnish.

Taste and adjust seasonings:
If you want it to have a saltier taste add a bit more fish sauce. To cut on the sour

note, add more sugar.

Prepare lettuce as your wrap. Remove 10-12 leaves from the stalk. Cut the tops of the leaf, leaving behind 3-4 inch pieces as your wrap. Place 1 teaspoon of the shrimp mixture into the middle of the lettuce leaf. Wrap by rolling the outer edges of the leaf as you would a tortilla. Set rolls on plate, garnish with cilantro leaves and toasted coconut, arranging with lime wedges.

Chapter 6: Side Dishes

How to Cook Rice

Investing in a rice cooker is worth losing counter space in my opinion. But you can also prepare rice on the stovetop and microwave if you're looking for convenience. Some of the finer points cooking the rice are in the preparation, which entails rinsing the rice a few times before cooking it. And as always, the best thing to do with rice before cooking is to soak it properly to remove lectins which can upset your gut. You can find the particular instructions for any strain of rice you have on the internet.

Step one: rinse the rice with cold water, swirling the rice kernels to wash off the starches, picking out any foreign objects (good to do even after soaking). This step allows for a finer texture in the cooked rice.

Next comes the cooking. Stovetop method entails boiling salted water, adding the rice, letting the mixture come to a boil, then covering and simmering until the water is absorbed. Usually directions on the bag of rice follow this method.

Stovetop Rice

Ingredients
2 cups	Water
1 cup	Rinsed long grain rice
¼ tsp.	Sea salt

Rinse and prepare rice as mentioned above. Place water in a 2-quart pot with a tight fitting lid. Heat water until it boils. Add rinsed rice, salt and stir. Allow the contents to return to a boil. Cover pot, reduce heat to a simmer, and allow rice to cook and absorb water. Most white, or jasmine rice takes 15-20 minutes to cook. Brown rice takes closer to 45 minutes to cook. Fluff rice with a fork before serving.

Microwave cooking is not going to save much time versus a rice cooker, or stovetop method. You will need a large glass container, with room for the rice to expand during the cooking process.

Microwave Cooked Rice

Ingredients
2 cups   Rinsed long grain rice
3 1/2 cups Water
1 1/2 tsp.   Butter or oil
Salt and pepper to taste.

Start with placing the rice, water, and oil in a large glass bowl or container. Cook on high for 10 minutes, and then reduce power to medium-low continuing to cook uncovered for 15 more minutes.

Do not stir the rice during the cooking process.

When time in the microwave is completed, fluff the rice with a fork and season with salt and pepper.

Coconut Rice

Coconut milk and coconut oil are becoming popular as a source of healthy fats. As endurance athletes, these types of fat deliver longer sustaining sources of energy. Coconut rice is popular in island and Latin American cooking and works well as a complement to curry dishes. The following recipe uses brown rice.

Ingredients
1 1/2 cups Brown jasmine or basmati rice
2 cups   Coconut milk
2 cups   Water
1/2 tsp.   Salt
3 Tbsp.   Dry shredded coconut
1 Tb.   Coconut oil, or other vegetable oil

Preparation

Use a 2-quart pan with a tight fitting lid. Measure and pour water in pan, allowing the water to boil before adding the rice, coconut milk, water, oil, and salt. Let the contents boil for 1 minute, then turn heat down to low, cover and simmer for up to 1 hour, until the coconut milk and water have been absorbed. When all (or nearly all) of the coconut-water is gone, turn off the heat and stir in shredded coconut, fluff the rice, and cover pot and let sit for 5-10 minutes before serving.

Basic Polenta

Polenta is a basic "gruel" made with corn, a bit of salt, butter, and water. It is also known as "grits" down south. When cooked to a looser consistency it can be an excellent substitute for mashed potatoes.

Cooked down to a thicker consistency, cooked polenta can be cut into pieces, garnished with cheese, placed under a broiler for a few minutes. If you are looking for a wheat free alternative to "pasta carbs" polenta can be used as a substitute lasagna noodle.

Ingredients
4 cups   Water
1 cup   Cornmeal or polenta
1 tsp.   Salt
1 Tb.   Unsalted butter

In a medium sized saucepan, heat up the 3 cups of water, reserving 1 cup. Add salt to the water and heat to a boil. With the cooler reserved water, mix the cornmeal in a small bowl or liquid measuring cup; add a bit of the hot water from the saucepan. Gradually drop in the mixture of cornmeal and water to the pot, stirring constantly to prevent clumping. Keep mixing over heat until the polenta gets thick. When bubbles start forming and popping, reduce to medium-high heat. Add butter, and continue mixing until ingredients are well integrated. Total cooking time can vary from 10 minutes on up—depending on the grind of cornmeal you are using, and the desired texture of the final product. The longer you cook it, the thicker it will turn out.

Pour the polenta mixture into a shallow pan or in an 8" pie dish and let cool so that it becomes solid. From there you may serve it with optional cheese and seasonings. Serves 6.

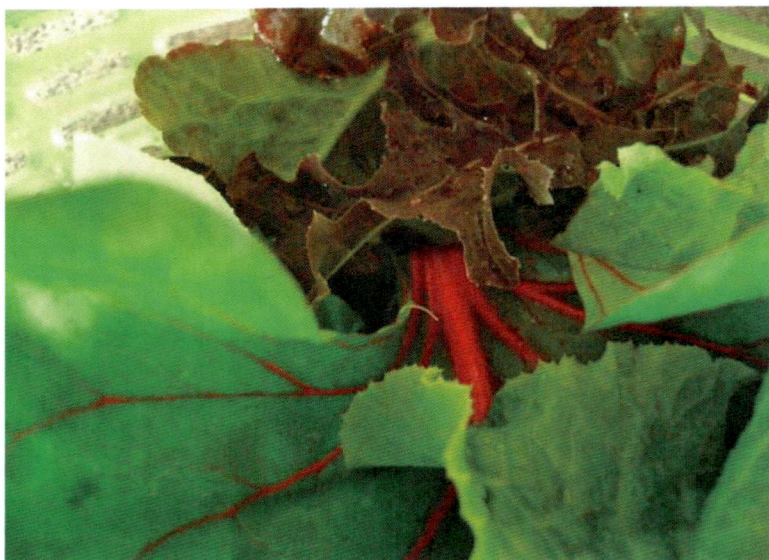

Anti-oxidant salad

This salad not only has excellent nutrition, featuring red cabbage, red onion and beets, but the intensity of the colors makes for a visual feast for the eyes. Mingling the tartness of the cabbage with the cilantro, a hint of citrus, and the nuttiness of sesame oil in the dressing makes for a dish that is as good for you as it is easy to look at. You can also substitute extra virgin olive oil for the sesame oil.

Ingredients

3 cups	Red cabbage thinly sliced as though making coleslaw
1 cup	Roasted or pickled beets chopped
1	Red onion diced, about 1/3 cup.
1/3-1/2 cup	Chopped cilantro
2 Tb.	Lemon or lime juice
¼ cup	Sesame oil
2	Cloves garlic finely minced
½ tsp.	Sea salt
¼ tsp.	Ground black pepper

Soak the red cabbage and red onion seperately in cold water for 4-8 hours before chopping. This will soften up the cabbage and take away the bite in the onion.

Next, combine the garlic, salt, pepper, lemon or lime juice, and sesame oil. Mix well and set aside as the dressing.
Mix chopped vegetables with the dressing and let sit at least 20 miuntes before serving.

Easy Barley Mushroom Pilaf

You need to plan ahead for this dish: give it about 1 hour of prep time in addition to soaking the barley. If you can afford the time it's easy to prepare. The cooking time of barley is 50 minutes, plus the 10 minutes needed for the mushrooms to gently cook. The barley is a hearty full textured grain that plays well with the meaty taste of the mushrooms.

Ingredients
4 cups	water
¾ cup	barley
½ tsp.	sea salt
2	large portabella mushrooms, diced.

In a medium sized saucepan add water and salt, bringing the ingredients up to a boil on high. Add barley, allowing it to cook for a minute then reduce temperature to a simmer. Place lid on pan and continue cooking for 40 minutes.

Add mushrooms to the barley mix, and continue cooking with the lid on the pan for an additional 10-15 minutes until most of the liquid is absorbed. Let the barley sit for a few minutes before serving.

Beans

You'll get close to 3 times the amount of beans using dried as the cost for one can of beans. Not to mention the distinct taste, which is vastly superior in my opinion. Dry beans shouldn't be intimidating, they just take a bit of planning ahead. A few methods will be discussed using implements such as pressure cookers, slow cookers, and stovetop preparation. 1 cup of dried beans yields 2 cups cooked beans.

Soaking

No matter which method you decide to use, you will have to rinse and soak your beans first.

Start with a bag of dried beans of any variety. Rinse with cool water using a colander, check and remove any debris, skins, or odd-looking beans.

Set rinsed beans in a large bowl and fill with cold water, allowing 2 inches of water above the level of the beans. If you have hard water, add a pinch of baking soda to the soaking water.

Soak beans for a minimum for 4 hours, maximum for 24. If you are in a warm climate, soak the beans in the refrigerator. If you are working with red beans, change the water twice during the soaking period.

Preparation of Beans

• Pressure Cooker: fastest method.
Make sure your cooker is in good working order, that the seals are functioning properly and that you have the correct weight for the pressure regulator.

Fill the pot with your beans, draining out the old water. Add new water, about 1-11/2 inches above the level of the beans. Heat up the pan on the stove, when the water is approaching boiling, set the lid with weights and properly lock the lid. Allow the beans to cook until the weight starts to rock, cook beans for 4-7 minutes, depending on the size of the beans you are cooking. When cooking time has finished, turn off the heat and let the pot sit for a few minutes. To release the pressure, take the cooker to the sink and rinse in cool water, so that the pressure seals release, allowing you to remove your cooked beans. Do not add salt to beans until they are finished cooking.

• Slow Cooker: slowest method.
The slow cooker is liberating in that you can start cooking, leave for the day, and

when you return the dish will be finished. There's an added benefit for the environment in that slow cookers use less energy. Fill the cooker with fresh water and pre-soaked beans, allowing for 2 inches of water to clear the level of the beans. Cook on low for 6-8 hours. Beans will be soft when fully cooked. Drain off extra water. Do not add salt to beans until they are finished cooking.

• Stovetop: pretty slow, but you need to supervise the process.
One method entails cooking the beans in water brought up to a boil, and then allowing it to sit for a few hours to soften. Rinse out the cooking water and simmer in ingredients such as vegetables and seasonings afterwards.

Slow method entails cooking the beans covered with 2 inches of water for an extended amount of time, up to an hour or more, until the beans are soft. Drain out the cooking water before serving.

Savory Beans

You can build an entire meal around this dish. If you are vegan, combining rice with beans provides a complete protein. Mixing and reheating left over beans and rice along with additional vegetables makes a satisfying meal, especially with a side of fried eggs. Allowing the beans to "rest" a day allows for the flavors to mingle and improves the taste.

Ingredients

2 Tb.	Oil, or butter
4 cups	Cooked Red or Kidney beans
14 ounce can	Diced, crushed, or stewed tomatoes
1	Medium onion, diced
3	Cloves diced garlic
2 tsp.	Ground cumin
1 tsp.	Mexican oregano
1 tsp.	Chili powder
½ tsp.	Ground black pepper
2 tsp.	Sea salt

Prepare beans using the methods above, or substitute with 2 cans of canned beans.

Heat oil over in a large pot over medium heat. Test the oil by dipping a piece of onion in the oil—if the onion sizzles, the pan is warm enough to start cooking your vegetables.

Add onions to the hot oil, cooking them for 3-5 minutes until they turn translucent. Add the garlic, making sure to stir the ingredients to prevent over-cooking. Continue to sauté the onions and garlic for 2-3 minutes. Add the cumin, Mexican oregano, chili powder, and black pepper, heating up the ingredients with the onions and garlic so that the flavors infuse.

Add the beans, salt, and diced tomatoes, stirring occasionally over medium heat. Continue cooking for 15-20 minutes or longer on medium to low heat. Avoid letting the mixture boil. Taste and correct seasonings before serving, adding more salt if needed.

Vegetables

In my coaching practice the routine with a new client entails going over the individual's food log. Sadly to say, much of the time exploring feeding habits has me sounding more like the client's mother encouraging the athlete to eat more vegetables. If you find yourself avoiding vegetables you aren't doing your performance any favors. Vegetables are rich in vital nutrients, and avoid the worry of taking in excess calories.

Why the resistance? If the taste of vegetables isn't your scene, then work on developing a taste by gradually by introducing new vegetables into your diet. Try different methods of preparing vegetables—especially if your negative experiences stemmed from eating mushy or flavorless overcooked vegetables. Avoid lengthy bouts with heat, or boiling vegetables, as it will reduce the nutritional value, as well as the flavor and textures.

For some, the taste of cruciferous vegetables such as cabbage, broccoli, cauliflower, kale, and Brussels sprouts can seem bitter. Rather than relying on sauces to cover up the sharp acid taste of these vegetables, try roasting them. Roasting transforms the food, giving these vegetables a whole new taste.

• Roasting
Roasting is a method used that will add interesting flavor to your vegetables, as the heat will caramelize the sugars found in the food.

To roast vegetables you will need a thick cookie or baking sheet with room enough to allow generous space between the vegetables, a source of heat such as an oven or grill, oil and seasonings. An easy way to season is freshly ground pepper and sea salt mixed with olive oil and lightly tossed before laying them out on the baking sheet. Check half way through cooking time to flip vegetables over.

Below is a table with guidelines on roasting vegetables.

Vegetable	Preparation	Temp	Time
Asparagus	whole	425°	10'
Beets	whole	450°	45-1 hour
Beets	sliced 1/4" pieces	425°	30-40'
Brussels Sprouts	halved	400°	15-20'
Carrots	cut in 1" pieces	425°	25-30'
Cauliflower	1-2" florets	400°	20-30'
Eggplant	1/2" wedges	425°	20-35'
Kale	leaves in 2" pieces	400°	15-20'
Sweet potato	1" wedges	400°	30-35'
Zucchini	quartered, 1" strips	425°	15-20'

Microwave Steaming of Vegetables

When time is tight, the microwave is an excellent way to speed up production. By using microwave safe cookware, such as Pyrex™ measuring cups, and wax paper, you can steam vegetables and retain more nutrients than boiling, or other stove top methods.

Start by placing your fresh or frozen vegetables in a microwave safe bowl or cooking implement such as a Pyrex liquid measuring cup (2 cup or 4 cup versions) and filling the bowl with water until it reaches about 1/2" from the bottom of the vessel. Using wax paper, create a cover for the dish so that steam stays within the dish. Cook in the microwave for 2 minutes or more, longer if cooking frozen vegetables, depending on the wattage of your microwave oven. Allow the wax paper to remain covering the dish for a few minutes, the steam inside will finish cooking the vegetables.

Root vegetables

The microwave also allows you to cook starchy vegetables without needing oil to prevent sticking.

How to do it:

Sweet potatoes: wrap in wax paper, using a piece that is long enough to securely wrap the ends around the potato and seal in the heat during cooking.

Cook for 4-5 minutes, then let them sit for a few minutes following the cooking, allowing the steam to fully cook the vegetables.

This method works well for yellow or ripe plantains (a tropical relative of the banana used in Caribbean and Latin cooking) as well, sparing the oil used for traditional frying methods. Keep the skin on and wrap in wax paper tightly. Microwave on full power for 5 minutes or longer. Allow time to steam and cool slightly before peeling off the skin and serving.

Baked Potatoes

Potatoes should be baked in the oven if you are looking to have fluffy textured potatoes. Preheat oven to 350°. Wash potatoes gently with a soft brush and remove any sprouts, or dark spots. Using a fork, poke a few holes in each potato so it won't burst in the oven during cooking. Depending on the size of your potato, you will need to bake it for an hour or longer. Check to see if the potato is ready by squeezing it, or sticking a fork in it. If the potato yields under pressure, and the skin is slightly crispy it is cooked.

Stuffed potatoes make a light meal. If you stuff a baked potato with prepared chicken or tuna salad, along with a nutritious vegetable such as spinach, peppers, alfalfa sprouts, broccoli, or roasted garlic you'll have a good meal.

Chapter 7: Dressings and Sauces

If you examine the nutritional content of store bought sauces you will notice "extras" such as corn syrup, preservatives, gluten, and high levels of salt. Preparing your own is satisfying and will open up opportunities to explore new tastes.

Aerobic Salad Dressing

Contains a balance of beneficial fats needed as fuel for long duration moderate to low intensity workouts.

Ingredients
4 oz.   Extra Virgin olive oil
4 oz.   Sesame oil
2 oz.   Apple cider vinegar
2 tsp. Sea salt
2   Cloves garlic diced
1 tbsp.   Dried parsley
2 tsp. Dried mustard.

Measure out liquid ingredients using a liquid measuring cup and pour into a carafe or jar which can sealed. Finely chop garlic, add parsley, sea salt, dried mustard and remaining ingredients into mixture. Mix well before serving. Store salad dressing refrigerator up to 3 weeks.

Provençal Sauce

Summer lends itself to this sauce when local farmers markets produce fresh tomatoes, or our gardens start to yield tomatoes. This sauce made from fresh tomatoes, herbs, as well as onion and garlic. Works well as a sauce for Italian dishes. You'll need a heavy pot to simmer the vegetables and preparation time of an hour to allow the flavors to mingle. Yields 6 cups.

Freeze what you don't use right away.

Ingredients
1 cup   Chopped onion
2-4   Minced garlic cloves
1/3 cup   Olive oil
2   Bay leaves
6 cups   Chopped fresh tomatoes
1 tsp.   Salt
1/4-1/2 tsp.   Ground fresh pepper, to taste
4-6   Springs fresh thyme, or about 1/4 tsp. dried
2 Tb.   Fresh marjoram, about 2 tsp. dried
2 Tb.   Tomato paste

Heat up a "heavy-sided" pot with olive oil. Add the onions and sauté until they become translucent; add garlic and bay leaf, continuing to cook for a few minutes, allowing the bay leaf's flavor to be released. Add tomatoes, salt, pepper, thyme, and marjoram. Drop the heat down a bit and simmer the sauce for 20 minutes. Add tomato paste and continue to cook for another 10 minutes. Taste the sauce making corrections for the flavor, adding more salt if the mixture tastes too sweet, since the flavors of the tomatoes may vary.

Cream Sauces

A roux (pronounced, "rue") is a mixture of equal parts of butter and flour. It is the essential component of sauce or gravy, providing thickness and creamy texture.

The mother of all sauces, béchamel sauce, starts with a roux made with butter and flour combined with cream or milk. From there sauce can be infinitely customized via seasonings, and cooking methods. Some varieties that start from béchamel sauce include mornay sauce using cheese, mustard sauce, and herb sauce.

How to do it:

To make roughly 1 cup start with:

2 Tb.	Butter
2 Tb.	All purpose flour, or rice flour
1 1/4 cup	Milk
1/4 tsp.	Salt
1/4 tsp.	Ground white pepper

Using a small saucepan with a heavy bottom melt the butter and add the flour over a low to medium-low heat. Mix the two ingredients together until it forms a paste. Add in very small amounts of milk and keep stirring using a wire whisk so the ingredients become integrated. Gradually add small amounts of milk, allowing the milk to heat and mix with the roux. Continue stirring, adding milk, letting it cook and allowing it to thicken after each addition. When the milk has been added, let the sauce continue to cook and thicken. Add salt, pepper, and mix until the desired thickness is achieved.

Variations:
• Add 1/4 tsp. dried mustard
• Add 1/4 tsp. dried nutmeg for Italian dishes such as lasagna, Greek Moussaka, or with green leafy vegetables such as spinach and kale.
• Add 1/4 dried mustard, 1/2 cup grated cheese plus a dash of Worcestershire sauce to make Mornay sauce.

Chapter 8: Main Courses

Food fuels us. It also takes our senses on a journey covering landscapes of tastes and textures. But despite the potential finesse, cooking with flavor need not be complicated. One of my favorite time saving and straight-forward methods is using rubs on meat. You can use rubs to shorten the time needed to infuse flavor in meat versus working with a marinade. Rubs are easy to prepare—you just need to combine ingredients in a small bowl. If available, use a pestle to break down the herbs and spices. Store in a cool, dark place in an airtight jar.

Jerk Seasoning

"Jerk" originates in Jamaica and the Caribbean Islands. This version is a bit tame, shying away from using the incredibly powerful varieties of peppers common in Caribbean culture, such as the scotch bonnet pepper. Feel free to include the extra heat if you can handle it, replacing the cayenne pepper.

2 Tb. Dried minced onion
2 1/2 tsp. Dried thyme
2 tsp. Ground allspice
2 tsp. Ground black pepper
1/2 tsp.   Ground cinnamon
1/2 tsp.   Cayenne pepper
1 tsp. Sea salt

Blackening Rub

Smokey flavor with some fire to go along with it. Works with meat, fish, and poultry.

2/3 cup	Chili powder
1/2 tsp.	Ground allspice
1/2 tsp.	Ground cayenne pepper, or smoked chipotle pepper
1 tsp.	Ground coriander
1 tsp.	Ground cumin
1 tsp.	Mexican oregano
1 tsp.	Ground black pepper

Poultry Rub

Use on chicken then grill or roast in the oven at 375° until fully cooked.

1 tsp.	Dried thyme
1 tsp.	Dried rosemary
1/2 tsp.	Dried sage
1/2 tsp.	Died marjoram
1 tsp.	Sea salt
1 tsp.	Coarsely ground black pepper

Break down the herbs by crumbing them first by hand, or using a mortar and pestle to integrate the herbs, salt, and pepper.

Barbecue Rub

1 Tb.	Paprika
1 tsp.	Sea salt
1 tsp.	Ground black pepper
1 tsp.	Ground ginger
1 tsp.	Ground cayenne pepper
1/2 tsp.	Ground dried garlic or garlic powder
1/2 tsp.	Dried thyme

Lamb Rub

1 tsp.	Ground dried mint
1 tsp.	Ground coriander
1 tsp.	Garlic powder
1 tsp.	Ground pepper
1/2 tsp.	Sea salt
1/2 tsp.	Dried rosemary
1/4 tsp.	Lemon rind

Skirt Steak

If you are fortunate enough to have skirt steak available, grab the opportunity to try this variety of flat steak. Similar to flank steak, skirt steak is a long and thin cut from the "plate" of beef. Skirt steak is well marbled, and can be tough (if done incorrectly), but is packed full of delicious flavor. If a grass fed option is available, the taste will be even better.

A skirt steak from a mature animal can reach the length that exceeds your grill, or broiler pan. Make sure you have the ability to cook the meat laid out flat, or just cut it into smaller more manageable pieces.

Two ways will be shown here: one is to marinade the meat, which requires working ahead of preparation time, and the other uses a rub in conjunction with meat tenderizer.

Some butchers may already have tenderized the meat so you might want to ask them when making your purchase. It's a bit of information that is not openly advertised.

If skirt steak in unavailable, the following cooking methods work as well on flank steak, which is a leaner cut. After cooking and resting the meat, make sure to cut flank steak in thin strips across the grain of the muscle fibers, making the meat more tender and easier to eat.

Skirt Steak Prepared with a Marinade

Have on hand a long but shallow dish, or a large sealable plastic bag.

In a small bowl combine the marinade:

3   Cloves minced garlic
½ tsp.   Salt
½ tsp.   Mexican oregano
1 tsp.Ground cumin
½ tsp.   Freshly ground black pepper
2 Tb. Worcestershire sauce
2 Tb. Olive oil
1 Tb Lemon juice (about ½ lemon)

Mix the ingredients, placing the meat into plastic bag or dish. Cover the meat on both sides with the marinate at least 1 hour to overnight before cooking in broiler, or on the grill using indirect heat.

Skirt Steak using a Rub

If you don't have the ability to marinade, a rub will impart flavor, pending you have tenderizer on hand. The longer you allow the rub to sit on the meat, the stronger the flavors will develop. Do not add salt in conjunction with use of meat tenderizer. Add salt to taste after the meat has been cooked.

Prepare the meat for the rub by using a fork to poke through the membrane on the outside of the skirt steak, allowing the holes to act as conduits for the tenderizer and rub to make it into the meat. Work your way across both sides of the meat. Sprinkle meat tenderizer over the meat according to the directions on the package. Set aside the meat and prepare the rub. In a small bowl combine:

¼ tsp.   Garlic powder
½ tsp.   Mexican oregano
½ tsp.   Freshly ground pepper
1 tsp. Ground cumin

Rub the mixture into the meat, massaging the rub into the grain of the muscle

Allow meat to stand at room temperature 15-20 minutes before cooking. This allows for easier cooking and more even heating throughout the cut of the meat.

Broil for 3-5 minutes on each side if using an oven, waiting until the meat starts brown up before flipping over to the other side. If grilling, avoid flare ups by placing coals on the outer perimeter of your grill, and allow the coals to burn down so that they are glowing. Place the meat in the center portion of your grill, away from the fire.

Check to make sure the meat is done by using a meat thermometer, or by piercing the meat with a knife tip. If clear juices run out, the meat is done. Cook to your preference, taking note that the thicker portions of meat requires longer cooking times than the thinner tapered ends of the skirt steak.

Let meat stand at least 5 minutes before serving.

Meatloaf

Unlike most meatloaf recipes, which uses crushed bread crumbs as the binding agent to give it its shape, this version uses crumbled up blue corn chips. Add diced green olives to the mix for a snappier version of an old standard. Have on hand a mixing bowl and a bread pan for cooking. If you are using spicy chips, omit the chili powder and pepper.
Preheat oven to 350°.

Ingredients
1 1/4 lb.   Ground sirloin, or bison meat
3/4 cup   Ground blue corn chips
2 1/2 tsp.   Chili powder (omit if your corn chips are seasoned)
1/2 tsp.   Cayenne, chipotle, adobo, another type of hot pepper
1 tsp.Mexican oregano
1/2 tsp.   Dried garlic powder or 3 minced cloves of garlic
1/2 cup   Minced onion
1   Egg beaten slightly
24   Medium sized green olives diced
1 Tb. Worcestershire sauce
1/2 cup   Milk

Mix ingredients well, integrating the dry and wet ingredients using a large spoon. Form into a loaf that is uniform in thickness to ensure even cooking. Place loaf in a greased pan. Bake in the lower two-thirds of the oven until internal temperatures reaches 140°, about 40-50 minutes. Let stand for 5 minutes before slicing and serving.

Quick and Easy No Fail Salmon

This method is an easy way to prepare salmon in the oven. No pots needed, and clean up is less complicated since the fish is cooked using aluminum foil. This works in the oven or over indirect heat in the grill. Leftovers can be used for fish tacos, tossed in with scrambled eggs, or mixed with mayonnaise as a sandwich spread. You may season the fish with the other spice mixes or rubs in this book such as the blackening rub or jerk seasoning.

Ingredients
1/2 lb.   Salmon fillet per serving
1/4 tsp.   Dried mustard

1/2 tsp.	Ginger powder
1 clove	Finely minced garlic
1/4 tsp.	Grated lemon peel
1 Tb.	Olive oil

Preparation

Preheat oven to 400° place rack on upper 1/3 of the oven.

In a small bowl or ramekin mix the dried seasonings and chopped garlic.

Start with a fresh salmon fillet. Allow 1/2 pound per person. Rinse and pat dry. Prepare a sheet of aluminum foil with 3 inches larger per side than the fillet you are working with in width and depth. Place salmon on the dull side of the foil, skin facing down. Rub the mixture of dried herbs into the muscle fibers, distributing evenly along the fillet. Drizzle olive oil over the fish. Grate with black pepper and sprinkle with a pinch of salt.

Wrap up the sides of the foil securely, folding over the edges twice or as many times required to swaddle the fish. Allow some space for air inside, leaving about 1/4 inch leeway. Fold over the ends, end over end until the foil is about 1/2" from the edge of the fillet. Package should be airtight, and leak proof. If you punctured the foil, set the fish on a baking sheet first to catch any drips.

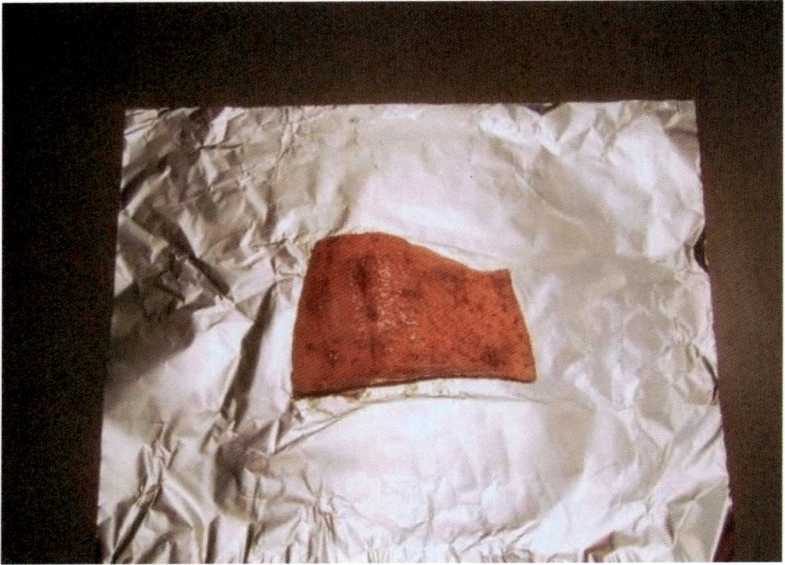

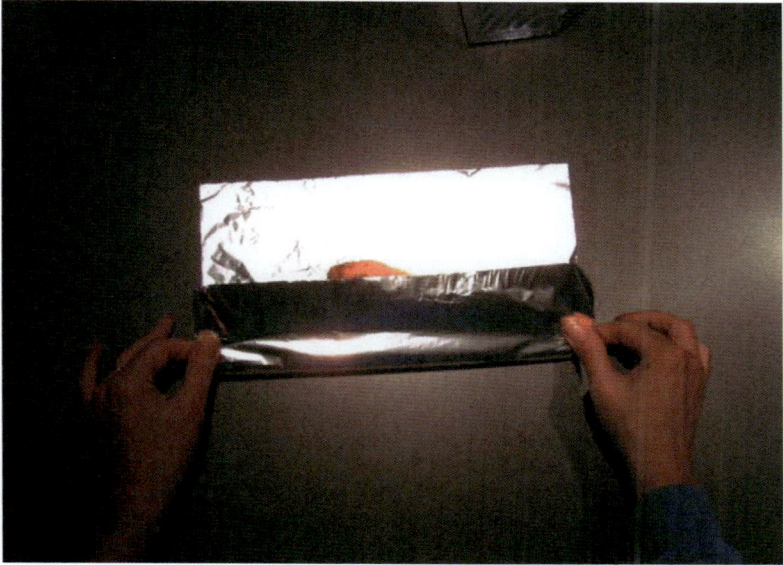

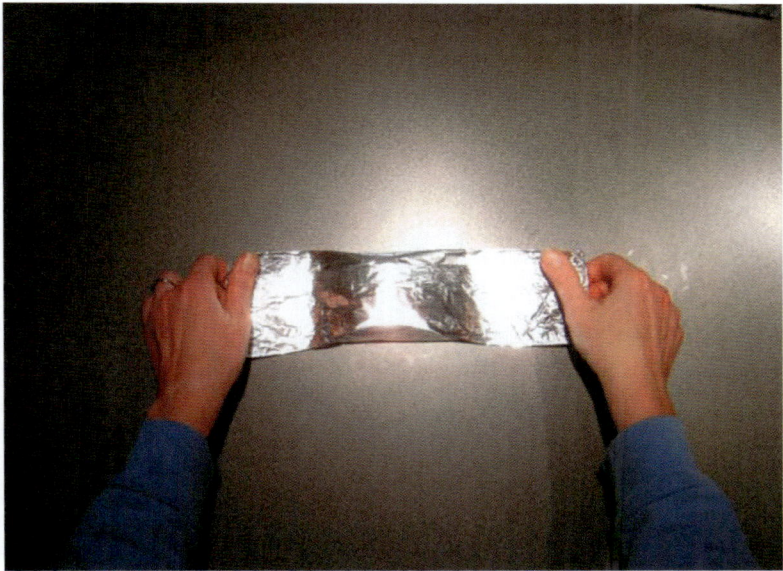

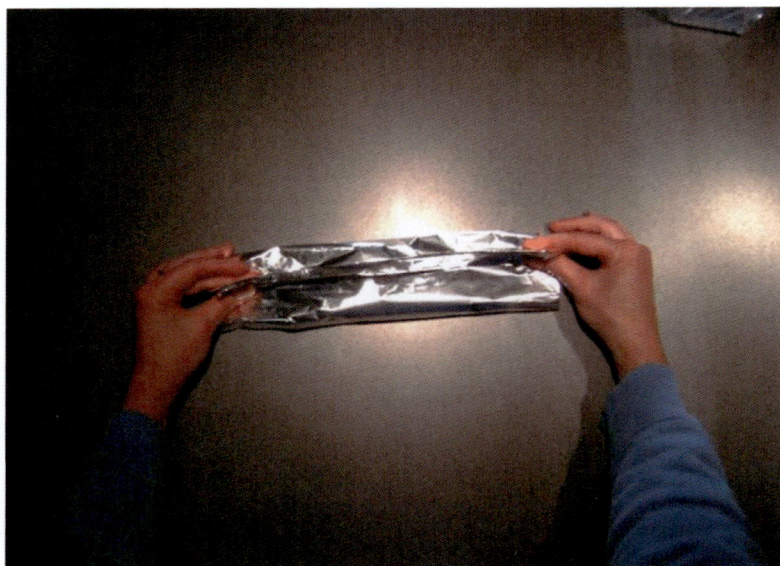

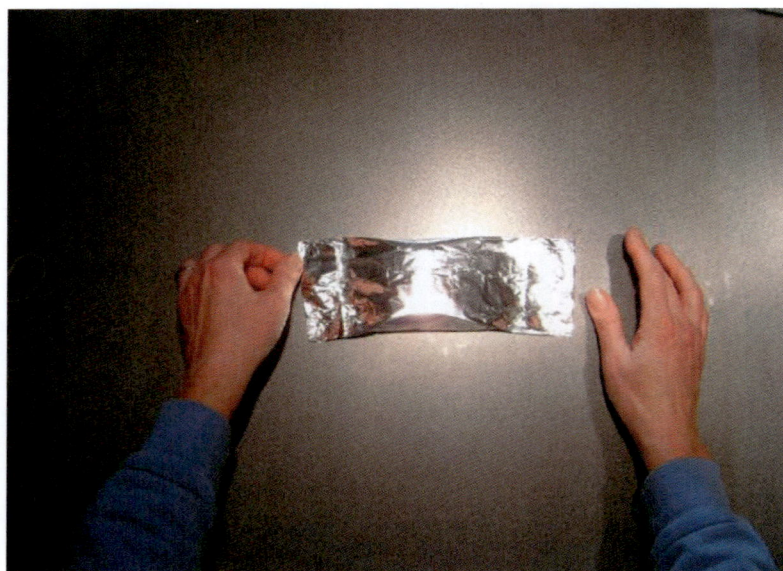

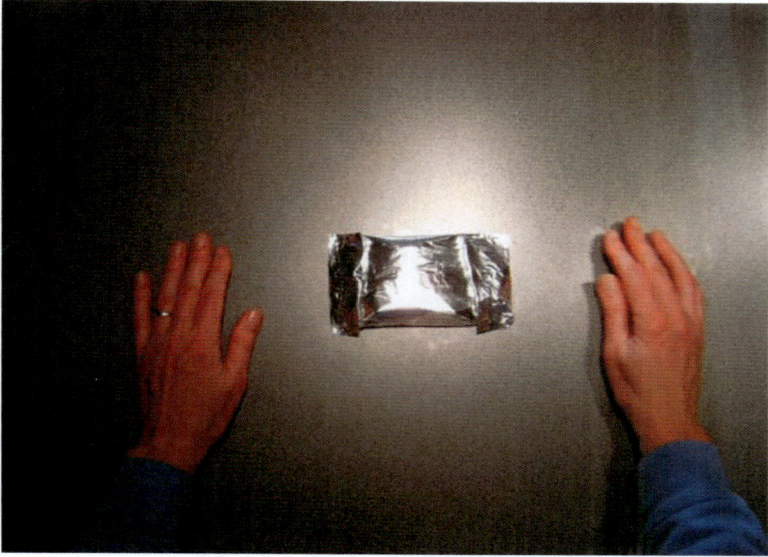

Place the foil wrapped fish in the oven. Cook 20 minutes per inch of thickness in the fillet. Check to see if the fish is done by opening up the foil, and testing the meat with a fork. If the sections of meat flake apart and are lighter in color compared to raw, the fish is done. Allow the fish to steam for a few minutes before removing from the foil and serving.

Black Bean and Salmon Tostadas

A healthy way to get in fiber and healthy fats with high quality protein in salmon, combined with avocado seasoned with some heat from jalapeno peppers. You can use leftover baked salmon using the "No Fail Salmon" recipe above.
Sliced cabbage and smoothly processed beans provide interesting texture.

Ingredients
8	6-inch corn tortillas
1	6-ounce can boneless, skinless wild Alaskan salmon, drained, or freshly baked salmon.
1	Avocado, diced
2 Tb.	Minced pickled jalapeños
1-2 Tb.	Lime juice
1-2 cups	Thinly sliced cabbage
2 Tb.	Chopped cilantro
15-oz	black beans, rinsed
3 Tb.	Sour cream (optional)
2 Tb.	Prepared salsa
2	Scallions, chopped
Lime wedges	(optional)

Start with the cabbage, chopping it into thin shredded pieces using a long sharp knife. Mix cabbage, cilantro and the lime juice in a bowl and set aside.

Position racks in upper and lower thirds of the oven; preheat to 350°F.

Brush both sides of tortillas with olive oil.

Place tortillas on baking sheets, and place in the oven. After 5 minutes, flip the tortillas over and bake for another 4-5 minutes, until they start to brown.

In a food processor, blend black beans, sour cream, salsa, and scallions until smooth. Transfer the mixture to a microwave-safe glass bowl. Cover with wax paper or paper towel and microwave on medium high until hot, about 3 minutes.

Prepare the fish by mixing the salmon, avocado and jalapeños in a bowl with a fork.

Assemble tostadas, spread each tortilla with some bean mixture and some salmon mixture and top with the cabbage salad. Serve with lime wedges, if desired.

One Pot Cajun Chicken Thighs

This complete meal-in-a bowl features a bit of fire with spicy ingredients, and some added kick from the flavors of Andouille sausages. With cannellini beans, carrots, peppers, and kale, this dish is packed with nutrition as well as taste. Serve with rice, polenta, or corn bread.

Ingredients

1 ½ lbs.	Chicken thighs, with or without the skin
4 cups	Chicken stock
2 Tb.	Olive oil, or butter
1	Can Cannellini (white) beans
2	Chopped carrots
½	Yellow, orange, red or green bell pepper, chopped
½	Medium onion
3	Cloves garlic, minced
2 tsp.	Smoked paprika
½ tsp.	Ground black pepper
½-1 tsp.	Cayenne pepper, to taste
1 tsp.	Dried thyme
1 lb.	Andouille Sausage, cut into ½ inch pieces.
¼ cup	Wheat or rice flour

½ lb.   Kale, mustard greens, chard, cut into ½ pieces or fresh spinach
2 Tb.   Juice of lemon or lime
Salt to taste

In a medium bowl, combine the flour, paprika, black pepper, cayenne pepper, and thyme. Dredge the pieces of chicken in the seasoned flour and set aside.

Preheat a large pot on medium to medium-high heat. Sear both sides of the chicken by cooking for 2-3 minutes per side, allowing the meat to brown. You may need to cook the chicken in separate batches if the chicken pieces are unable to sit on the bottom of the pan all at once.
Add the sausage, onions, garlic, peppers, and carrots, stirring frequently so that the vegetables cook, taking care not to burn the garlic. When the onion turns translucent, add the beans, chicken stock, remaining seasoned flour and cover with lid and cook for 20 minutes on medium heat, stirring on occasions.

Test the soup to see if additional salt is needed and correct the seasonings. Add the kale, or greens and cook with the lid on for an additional 10 minutes, or until the greens are soft. Before serving, add the juice of lemon or lime to the pot, and stir through. Serve in bowls.

Pollo â la Plancha (Grilled chicken with carmelized onions)

Serves 4.

Ingredients

4 breast	Skinless, boneless chicken
2	Cloves chopped garlic
1	Medium onion cut into rings
1/3 cup	Chopped cilantro
1	Lemon
	Hot sauce (to season according to taste)
	Sea salt and ground pepper
2 tbsp. chicken	Butter, or olive oil for sautéing

Using a hammer or frying pan, tenderize chicken by placing the breasts inside a 18" piece of freezer paper folded in half or freezer bag and pounding on the covered chicken breast until the thickest part of the chicken is about ½ inch thick and uniform in thickness. This process will tenderize the chicken and allow it to cook faster.

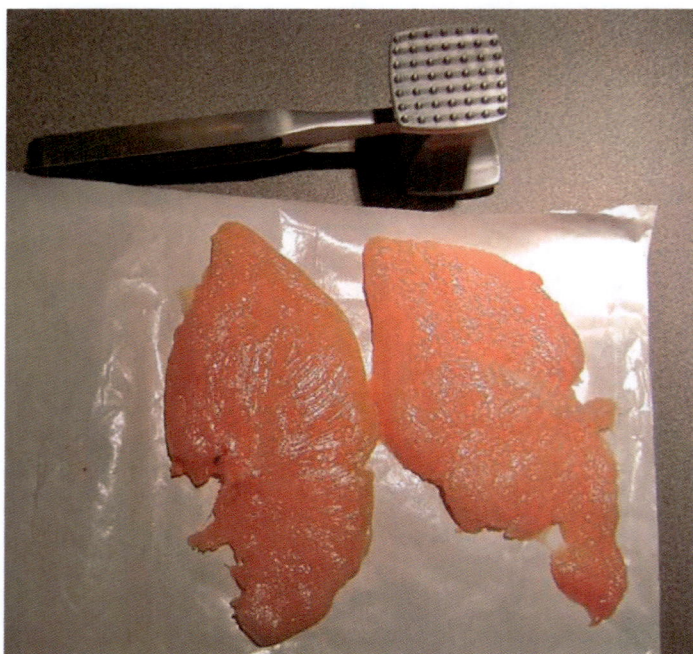

Season breasts with a light coating of salt and ground pepper on both sides then set aside. Chop cilantro and cut onion into rings by slicing across the onion. Squeeze lemon and set aside.

Preheat a large (14" or larger) frying pan on medium high heat. Test the pan for readiness by dropping a few drops of water on the pan. If the water sizzles quickly (dances), the pan is ready for the oil.
Coat the pan with oil/butter, allowing it to heat up. Check the fat by testing with a piece of onion. If the onion starts cooking and sizzling the fat is ready. Do not overheat the oil/butter.

Start cooking by sautéing the onion until translucent, then move the onions to the sides of the pan to make room for the chicken.

Place chicken in the pan, using a spatula, or lid from a smaller pan press the chicken into the pan to sear on medium-high heat. Cook 2-3 minutes per side, and then add garlic, continuing to move the vegetables so that they do not overcook. Reduce the heat to medium, and continue cooking until the chicken is done. Test by using a meat thermometer to 150°, or by piercing the chicken with a knife. If the breast produces clear liquid, the meat is cooked. Just before serving, add the cilantro, then lemon juice and hot sauce and continue to cook for 1-3'.

This dish makes an excellent meal if served with cooked brown rice and black beans.

Hunter Chicken

Imagine being outdoors for most of a chilly autumn day in pursuit of wild game, or just being out for a long ride or trail run on a fall day when the ground is littered with fallen leaves. You become aware of the shift in the seasons, and the food on the dining table moves away from lighter fare to more substantial meals that warm you up. If you canned some homegrown tomatoes, and had some fresh thyme, this dish will showcase your summer harvest too.

This savory dish features chicken cooked up with a variety of vegetables, including tomatoes, mushrooms, artichokes, and kalamata olives. Serve with a grain or small sized pasta such as orzo as side dish to absorb and blend with the savory chicken broth.

To prepare this dish, you will start with braising the chicken on a skillet, and sautéing the vegetables before combining the ingredients and baking the ensemble in the oven. This dish comes out with tender chicken in a tomato sauce, surrounded by the tantalizing combination of the briny olives, smoky mushrooms, with the tartness of the artichokes.

Preparation time: 50 minutes, 1 hour cooking time. This dish reheats well in the oven if you were to make it a day ahead.

Ingredients:
1 ¼ teaspoon each of:
                    Dried Mexican oregano,
dried thyme, salt, freshly ground pepper
1/3 cup   Rice flour
8   Chicken thighs
1   Diced red onion, about 1 ½ cups
3-5   Cloves of garlic finely diced
3-4   Large portabella mushrooms
chopped into ¼" squares, or about ½ cup
                    smaller mushroom variety.
12   Kalamata olives sliced
1   Can quartered artichokes
3-5 Tb.   Olive oil
½ cup   Dry white wine or vermouth
1   14 ounce can diced
tomatoes plus juice
2 Tb.   Tomato paste
¼ cup   Dry white wine

Preheat oven to 375 with the rack set at the lower 1/3 of the oven. While preparing the chopped vegetables, preheat a large 12-14" skillet or sauté pan to braise the chicken. Dredge the chicken in the flour and herb mix. Find a shallow baking dish that is large enough to accommodate the chicken without being crammed into dish.

Combine the dried herbs, flour, salt and pepper in a bag sturdy enough and large enough to contain 1-2 chicken thighs. Add chicken pieces into the bag containing the herb and flour mix and shake until chicken is covered in mix. Do this for all the chicken thighs.

Heat 2 tablespoons olive oil in the sauté pan over medium high heat. Place the coated chicken in the hot oil and brown the chicken by cooking for 3-4 minutes per side. Braise the chicken in a few batches this way, placing the braised chicken on the shallow baking pan.

Add the remaining oil to the pan once the chicken has been prepared. Start with sautéing the onions and mushrooms first, and when they start releasing some moisture, add the garlic and continue to cook, about 4 minutes until the onion are softened. Sprinkle the remaining flour and herb mixture from the bag and stir well. Add the remaining ingredients, stirring the mixture until it starts to boil. When the mixture starts to bubble, turn off the heat, and get ready to combine with the chicken.

Transfer the vegetables from the pan to the baking dish, covering the chicken. Cover the baking dish with foil and bake in the oven at 375°, checking to see if the chicken is cooking after 40 minutes. If the pan looks dry, add some water, a few ounces at a time. After the cooking time is up, let the dish sit for 5 minutes before serving.

Curry Pork and Eggplant

This makes a great summer dish when eggplant is in season.

Ingredients

1 Tb	Coconut oil/Butter
2 Tb.	Red, or green curry paste
1 1/2 lbs.	Ground pork
1	Large eggplant, cut into 1-inch pieces
1 ½ cup	Chicken broth
¾ cup	Coconut milk
1	Green onion or scallion thinly sliced
½ cup	Chopped fresh cilantro leaves

Brown meat in the fat, add eggplant, cook until soft. Add curry paste, chicken stock, and coconut milk and bring to boil, reduce heat, stirring until eggplant is tender and completely cooked, 10 minutes or longer. Add scallion, cilantro just before serving.

(Photo: Rebecca Palay)

What Is Endurance Planet?

Endurance Planet, the publisher of this book, is the premiere online destination for runners, cyclists, swimmers, triathletes, and adventure racers who want inspiration and education!

We provide several free audio podcasts each week, including episodes on sports nutrition, sports medicine, guest experts, and interviews with amateur and pro athletes who have compelling stories of endurance.

At EndurancePlanet.com, you will also find training videos and video interviews with endurance athletes, an endurance sports bookstore, and brand new technology that lets you share, upload and get points for your endurance efforts, whether you're a seasoned pro or you're just getting started.

If you visit EndurancePlanet.com today, you can also get access to free training plans via our weekly Endurance Planet newsletter!

ENDURANCE PLANET   How far can you go...

More from Endurance Planet…

No endurance athlete's library would be complete without Ben Greenfield's "Top 20 Fueling Myths Exposed" or Jeff Meador's "Guide To Elevation". Get both now at **EndurancePlanet.com/bookstore**

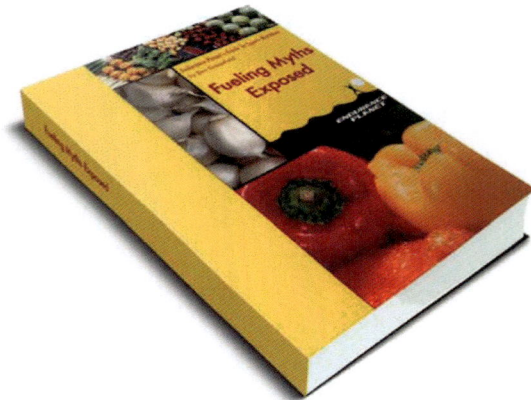

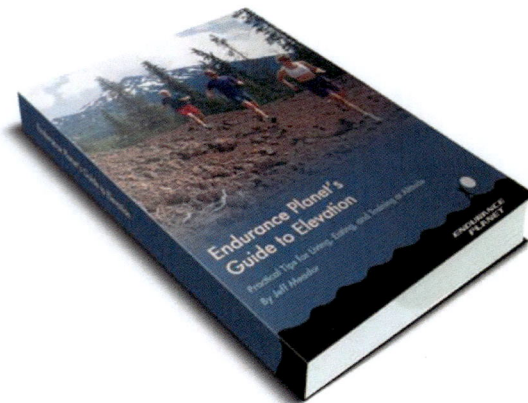

Printed in Germany
by Amazon Distribution
GmbH, Leipzig